TABLE OF CONTENTS

DISCLAIMER 4
CHAPTER ONE 6
INTRODUCTION 6
CHAPTER TWO 10
TECHNICAL SPECIFICATIONS 10
CHAPTER THREE 20
DESIGN AND BUILD QUALITY 20
CHAPTER FOUR 28
USER INTERFACE AND MENU SYSTEM 28
CHAPTER FIVE 36
RECORDING MODES AND OPTIONS 36
CHAPTER SIX 44
IMAGE STABILIZATION AND HANDLING 44
CHAPTER SEVEN 50
POWER AND BATTERY LIFE 50
CHAPTER EIGHT 58
CONNECTIVITY AND REMOTE CONTROL 58
CHAPTER NINE 66
ACCESSORIES AND COMPATIBILITY 66
CHAPTER TEN 76
WORKFLOW AND POST-PRODUCTION 76
CHAPTER ELEVEN 82
COMPARISON WITH OTHER CINEMA LINE CAMERAS 82
CHAPTER TWELVE 88
PROS AND CONS 88

SONY CINEMA LINE FX30 USER GUIDE

The Professional Handbook to Use this Compact Camera and Explore its Features

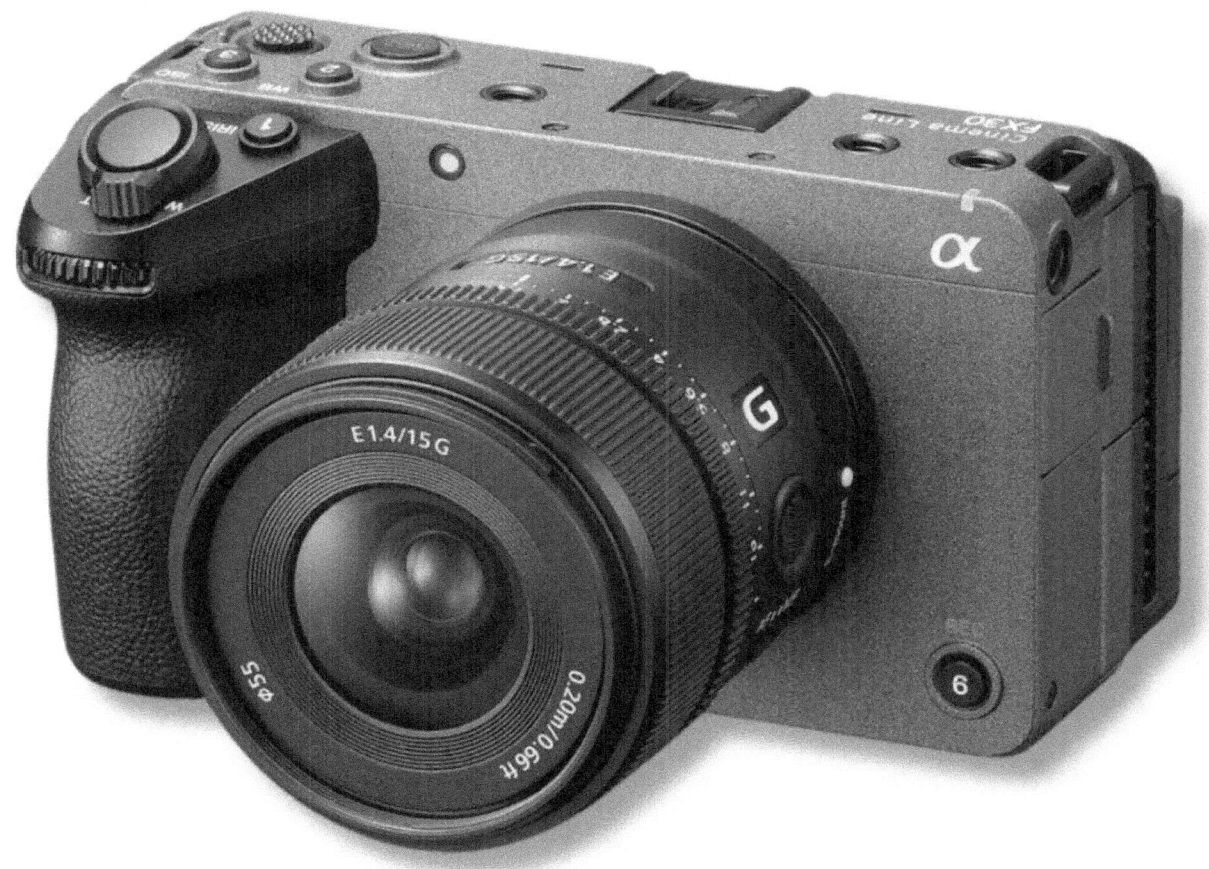

ALLEN DAVIS

Copyright © 2024 Allen Davis

Unauthorized reproduction, distribution, or transmission of any part of this publication in any form or by any means, including photocopying, recording, or other electronic or mechanical methods, without the prior written permission of the publisher, is prohibited. Brief quotations may be used in critical reviews and other non-commercial uses permitted by copyright law, provided proper attribution is given.

DISCLAIMER

The contents of this book are provided for informational and entertainment purposes only. The author and publisher do not make any representations or warranties regarding the accuracy, applicability, completeness, or suitability of the contents for any purpose.

The information in this book is based on the author's personal experiences, research, and opinions, and should not be considered a substitute for professional advice. Readers are advised to consult appropriate professionals regarding their specific situations.

The author and publisher are not liable for any loss, injury, or damage allegedly arising from the information or suggestions in this book. Any reliance on such information is at the reader's own risk.

The inclusion of third-party resources, websites, or references does not imply endorsement or responsibility for their content or services.

Readers are encouraged to use their own discretion and judgment when applying the information or recommendations in this book to their own lives.

All rights reserved. No part of this book may be reproduced, distributed, or transmitted in any form or by any means without the prior written permission of the publisher, except for brief quotations in critical reviews and certain other non-commercial uses permitted by copyright law.

Thank you for reading and understanding this disclaimer

CHAPTER ONE
INTRODUCTION

Overview of the FX30 Model

The Sony Cinema Line FX30 is a compact, entry-level cinema camera that brings the acclaimed features of Sony's Cinema Line series to a more accessible price range, making it an attractive choice for filmmakers, content creators, and aspiring cinematographers. Built with an emphasis on video production, the FX30 combines professional-grade features like high-resolution 4K recording, advanced colour profiles, and robust autofocus with a user-friendly design and compact form factor.

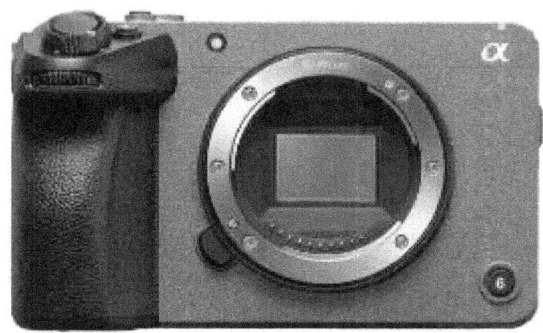

Key Highlights of the FX30:

- **4K Super 35 Sensor**: The FX30 is equipped with a Super 35 sensor capable of capturing 4K footage at up to 120fps, delivering stunning detail, dynamic range, and colour accuracy. This sensor size also offers a slight crop that can benefit depth of field control and low-light sensitivity, ideal for cinematic visuals.

- **Professional-Grade Colour Science**: The camera supports Sony's S-Cinetone colour science, inspired by the higher-end FX6 and FX9 models, which provides a rich, cinematic look straight out of the camera. It also supports 10-bit 4:2:2 recording, offering flexibility in post-production for colour grading and ensuring maximum colour accuracy

- **Compact and Lightweight Design**: The FX30 is designed to be highly portable and is smaller and lighter than most traditional cinema cameras, making it easy to use for handheld shooting, rigging on gimbals, or tight setups. Despite its compact size, it includes a rugged magnesium alloy body and improved heat dissipation to prevent overheating during prolonged shoots.

- **Fast and Reliable Autofocus**: Borrowing autofocus capabilities from Sony's Alpha series, the FX30 features Real-time Eye AF, Face Detection, and Object Tracking, ensuring smooth and accurate focus on subjects even in challenging conditions. This autofocus system is particularly helpful for solo shooters or in situations where manual focus may be challenging.

- **Dual-Base ISO and High Dynamic Range**: With dual-base ISO, the FX30 offers greater flexibility in various lighting conditions. It's optimized for both bright and low-light scenarios, making it possible to achieve high dynamic range and low noise levels, crucial for capturing detailed, high-quality footage.

- **Comprehensive Video Recording Options**: The FX30 supports internal 4K 10-bit recording at 4:2:2 colour depth, giving creators the ability to capture cinematic quality footage with excellent colour fidelity. It also allows for external RAW recording when paired with compatible devices, appealing to those seeking higher data rates for extensive post-processing.

- **Customizable and User-Friendly Interface**: The FX30's interface and button layout have been optimized for video production, with customizable buttons, an intuitive menu system, and a touchscreen LCD for easy navigation. The camera also has tally lights, commonly seen in cinema cameras, to indicate when recording is active.

- **Versatile Connectivity**: The FX30 offers multiple ports, including HDMI, USB-C, 3.5mm audio input, and microphone and headphone jacks, making it adaptable to a wide range of professional workflows. It also supports Wi-Fi and Bluetooth connectivity for remote control and monitoring through compatible devices and apps.

The Sony Cinema Line FX30 is a powerful choice for filmmakers who need a high-performance, versatile camera without the hefty price tag of higher-end cinema cameras. It's ideal for those seeking the flexibility of a professional-grade system but in a compact, mobile package suited for various shooting environments. This combination of features has made the FX30 popular in the world of indie filmmaking, content creation, and small-scale professional video production.

Target Audience and Use Cases

The Sony Cinema Line FX30 targets filmmakers and content creators who seek a cinema-grade camera without the high cost of more advanced models. Its features and design cater to a range of users in various fields, especially those looking for high-quality, versatile, and portable gear for video production. Here's a breakdown of the target audience and ideal use cases for the FX30:

Target Audience

1. **Independent Filmmakers and Cinematographers**:
   - Indie filmmakers often work on tight budgets and need high-quality equipment that can deliver cinematic results without requiring large crews. The FX30's professional-grade features, including 4K recording, dynamic range, and S-Cinetone colour science, offer a significant value proposition in a compact package.

2. **Content Creators and YouTubers**:
   - Many content creators are expanding into high-quality video production to stand out. With its intuitive design and ease of use, the FX30 is ideal for creators who prioritize image quality and need features like reliable autofocus, stabilization, and connectivity for livestreaming, vlogging, or tutorial videos.

3. **Documentary Filmmakers**:
   - Documentarians need versatile, durable, and portable equipment for shooting on location in various environments. The FX30's lightweight build, dual-base ISO for low-

light scenarios, and long recording times make it a suitable choice for filmmakers working on the go.

4. **Wedding and Event Videographers**:
   - For professionals who capture live events, the FX30's autofocus capabilities, long battery life, and high-quality 4K recording with good low-light performance are essential for capturing key moments in challenging conditions, from low-light receptions to fast-moving action on the dance floor.

5. **Corporate and Commercial Videographers**:
   - Many corporate clients demand high-quality video, and the FX30's professional look and extensive post-production flexibility make it an appealing choice for commercial and corporate projects. Its compact design is also ideal for shooting in various settings, from office interviews to industrial sites.

6. **Educational and Training Video Producers**:
   - For institutions and businesses that produce training materials or educational content, the FX30 provides high-quality visuals that improve viewer engagement. It's reliable, offers great colour reproduction, and has autofocus features that allow single operators to produce professional-looking videos.

Ideal Use Cases

1. **Narrative Film Projects**:
   - The FX30 is designed for cinematic productions with features that mimic traditional cinema cameras. Its 10-bit 4:2:2 recording and support for S-Log3 and S-Cinetone profiles make it capable of producing film-quality footage suitable for short films, web series, and independent films.

2. **YouTube and Social Media Content**:
   - Content creators who prioritize image quality will find the FX30 excellent for producing visually stunning videos, tutorials, or lifestyle vlogs. The camera's autofocus and compact size allow for flexibility in filming solo or with minimal crew.

3. **Documentary and Travel Filmmaking**:
   - For filmmakers capturing content in dynamic, real-world settings, the FX30's rugged design and portability make it easy to handle in the field. Its low-light performance and dual-base ISO enhance footage quality in varying lighting conditions, making it a reliable choice for travel and documentary work.

4. **Interviews and Corporate Videos**:
   - The FX30 is ideal for corporate interviews, product shoots, or branding videos. Its professional look, shallow depth of field, and reliable autofocus help create polished footage with a cinematic touch that aligns well with corporate standards.

5. **Event Videography (Weddings, Concerts, Live Performances)**:

- The FX30's autofocus, long recording times, and 4K resolution make it ideal for events. Whether capturing weddings, concerts, or live performances, the camera's colour accuracy, dynamic range, and low-light capability allow it to handle different lighting scenarios.

6. **Educational Content and Online Courses**:
    - Educators and online course creators can use the FX30 to produce professional-quality videos that enhance viewer engagement and learning. The camera's ease of use, long recording capabilities, and options for external audio make it perfect for filming lectures, tutorials, or instructional content.

7. **Multi-Camera Productions**:
    - Due to its size and price point, the FX30 is also well-suited as a secondary or tertiary camera in multi-camera setups, matching well with other Sony Cinema Line cameras in terms of colour science and quality. It works well for concert filming, conferences, and other live events where multiple angles are needed.

The Sony Cinema Line FX30 fits well within a variety of workflows, especially for those looking for a cost-effective, professional solution without sacrificing image quality. Its compact form, professional features, and adaptability to various shooting conditions make it an all-around performer for creators across multiple disciplines.

CHAPTER TWO
TECHNICAL SPECIFICATIONS

Sensor and Image Quality

The Sony FX30 uses a 4K Super 35 (APS-C size) sensor, delivering impressive image quality and flexibility for filmmakers. This sensor, paired with Sony's advanced image processing, provides high resolution, excellent colour reproduction, and dynamic range—qualities that are essential for achieving cinematic visuals. Here's how you can leverage the sensor and image quality to enhance your video projects:

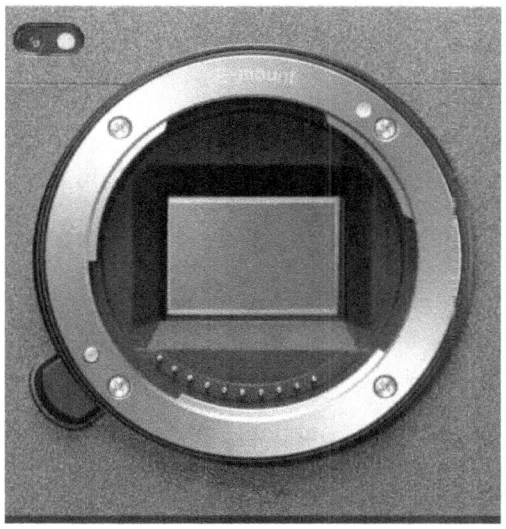

1. High-Resolution 4K Video

- **How to Use**: The FX30's Super 35 sensor captures 4K footage that is oversampled from a 6K sensor readout, providing detailed and crisp visuals. To maximize this feature, shoot in 4K resolution to ensure the highest quality for larger displays or for projects requiring heavy cropping in post-production without loss of detail.

- **Tip**: Use 4K when capturing establishing shots, scenic vistas, or any scene where detail is essential. Oversampled 4K provides a more natural look, perfect for professional-grade content.

2. Dual-Base ISO for Low Light and Bright Light Scenarios

- **How to Use**: The FX30's dual-base ISO feature enhances performance in both low-light and bright-light conditions. Set the base ISO according to your lighting: for daylight or well-lit conditions, use the lower base ISO, and for dimly lit environments, switch to the higher base ISO for optimal results.

- **Tip**: When shooting in low light, enable the higher base ISO to reduce noise and retain shadow detail. This is ideal for night scenes or dimly lit indoor settings.

3. Cinematic Colour Profiles (S-Cinetone and S-Log3)

- **How to Use**: The FX30 comes with S-Cinetone for immediate, cinematic colour out of the camera and supports S-Log3 for maximum control in post-production. S-Cinetone is perfect for projects requiring minimal colour grading, while S-Log3 is ideal for those needing extensive colour correction and dynamic range.
- **Tip**: For a fast turnaround, use S-Cinetone to achieve a professional look without grading. For more intensive projects, shoot in S-Log3 to give you flexibility in adjusting shadows, highlights, and colours in post.

4. High Dynamic Range (HDR) with HLG (Hybrid Log-Gamma)

- **How to Use**: HLG allows you to capture high dynamic range footage that looks more realistic, especially in scenes with contrasting bright and dark areas. HLG footage can be easily displayed on HDR-compatible devices, making it great for future-proofing content.
- **Tip**: Use HLG when shooting outdoor scenes with bright skies and dark foregrounds to capture detail across a wider exposure range. HLG footage can be used directly on HDR displays, saving time if you plan to distribute content on HDR-compatible platforms.

5. Frame Rate Flexibility for Slow Motion and Real-Time Recording

- **How to Use**: The FX30 supports high frame rates, including 4K at 60fps and Full HD at 120fps, ideal for capturing smooth slow-motion shots. These frame rates allow you to slow down action shots, adding dramatic emphasis to movement or enhancing storytelling.
- **Tip**: Use 120fps for slow-motion sequences, such as capturing water splashes, movement in sports, or expressive actions. For general scenes, use 24fps or 30fps for a natural look.

6. Rolling Shutter Control

- **How to Use**: The FX30's advanced sensor minimizes rolling shutter effects (jello effect) often seen in fast-moving shots. While this doesn't entirely eliminate rolling shutter, it reduces distortion when panning quickly or shooting action scenes.
- **Tip**: Use the FX30's fast sensor readout when shooting handheld or panning across scenes with fast-moving subjects to reduce wobble and skewing in your footage.

7. Shallow Depth of Field for Cinematic Looks

- **How to Use**: The Super 35 sensor offers a balance between depth of field and light-gathering capability. Combined with a wide aperture lens, you can create a shallow depth of field, achieving a cinematic look with sharp focus on the subject and a blurred background.
- **Tip**: For interviews, close-ups, or storytelling, use lenses with wide apertures (e.g., f/2.8 or wider) to isolate your subject against a soft, out-of-focus background, enhancing the cinematic feel.

8. Creative Flexibility with Interchangeable Lenses

- **How to Use**: The FX30 uses Sony's E-mount, compatible with a wide range of lenses. Selecting different lenses, from wide-angle to telephoto, allows you to control composition and narrative style.

- **Tip**: Use prime lenses for sharper images and natural light-gathering capability, and zoom lenses for versatility when quickly adjusting focal lengths on location.

The Sony FX30's sensor and image quality open up possibilities for crafting detailed, dynamic, and visually compelling video content. By utilizing its capabilities, you can achieve a professional and cinematic look that is adaptable to various storytelling styles.

Lens Compatibility and Mount

The Sony FX30 is designed to be compatible with a wide range of lenses, primarily utilizing the E-mount system. This flexibility allows users to enhance their photography and videography capabilities by choosing from various lens types, including prime, zoom, wide-angle, and macro lenses. Here's a detailed overview of how this functionality can be utilized.

Lens Types Compatible with Sony FX30

1. **APS-C Lenses**:

    - The FX30 is optimized for APS-C lenses, which are specifically crafted for its sensor size. These lenses provide excellent image quality and are lightweight, making them ideal for handheld shooting.

    - Examples include:

        - **Sony 16-55mm f/2.8 G**: A versatile zoom lens that excels in various shooting scenarios with fast autofocus and sharp image quality.

        - **Sigma 30mm f/1.4**: A budget-friendly prime lens known for its large aperture, making it perfect for low-light situations and achieving beautiful bokeh.

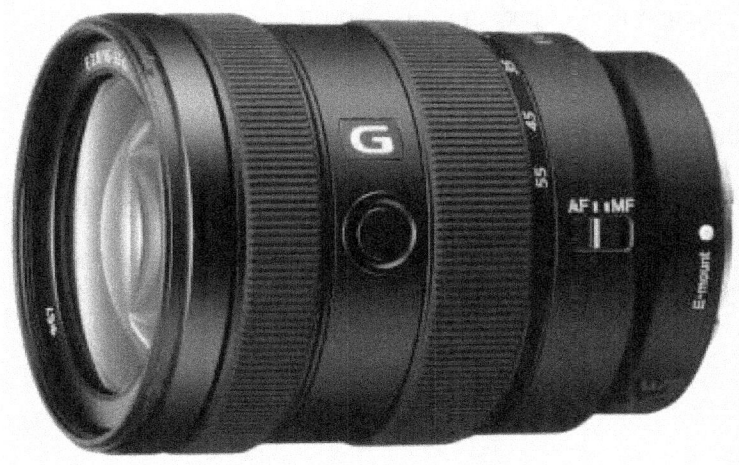

2. **Full-Frame Lenses**:
    - The FX30 can also use full-frame E-mount lenses. When these lenses are attached, the camera operates in a cropped mode, effectively utilizing the APS-C sensor while allowing for future upgrades to full-frame systems.
    - Notable full-frame options include:
        - **Sony 24mm f/1.4 GM**: Offers exceptional sharpness and low-light performance

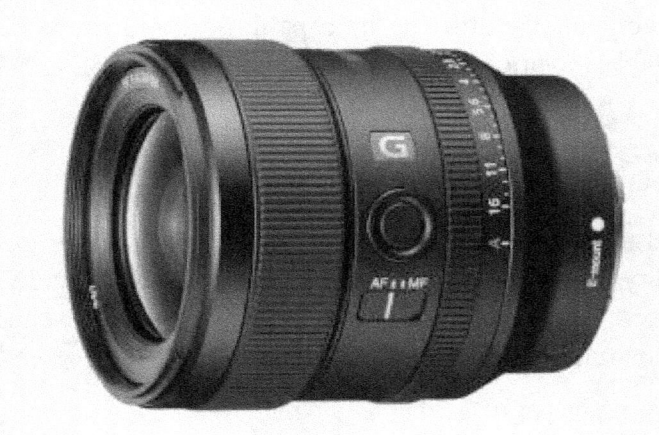

Vintage Lenses:

- With appropriate adapters, vintage lenses can be mounted on the FX30, expanding creative possibilities and enabling unique photographic styles.

Key Features of Lens Compatibility

- **Breathing Compensation**: Some compatible lenses support breathing compensation, which minimizes focus shifts during video recording, enhancing the cinematic quality of footage. This feature is beneficial for filmmakers looking to achieve smooth focus transitions.
- **Ease of Lens Change**: Changing lenses on the FX30 is straightforward:
    1. Turn off the camera to prevent dust from entering the sensor.
    2. Locate and press the lens release button near the lens mount.
    3. Rotate the lens counter-clockwise to detach it.
    4. Align the new lens with the mount markers and rotate clockwise until it clicks into place.

Practical Applications

- **Versatility in Shooting Scenarios**: The ability to use various lenses allows photographers and videographers to adapt to different environments and subjects, from landscapes to portraits.

- **Creative Exploration**: Utilizing vintage lenses or specialized macro lenses can lead to unique artistic expressions that standard modern lenses may not achieve.

- **Future-Proofing Equipment**: The compatibility with both APS-C and full-frame lenses means that users can invest in high-quality glass without worrying about obsolescence as they upgrade their camera systems.

In summary, the Sony FX30's E-mount compatibility provides extensive options for both amateur and professional users, enabling them to tailor their equipment to meet specific creative needs while ensuring high-quality results across various shooting conditions.

Recording Formats and Resolutions

The Sony Cinema Line FX30 supports a variety of recording formats and resolutions, making it a versatile tool for different types of video production. With options ranging from high-quality 4K to lower-resolution proxies, filmmakers have the flexibility to choose the format and resolution that best suit their project requirements. Here's an overview of the available options and guidance on how to use them effectively:

1. 4K UHD (3840 x 2160) Resolution

- **Recording Format**: The FX30 records 4K in XAVC S (standard), XAVC HS (high-efficiency), and XAVC S-I (intra-frame) formats.

- **Frame Rates**: 24, 30, and 60 fps; up to 120 fps in Full HD.

- **Use Case**: 4K UHD is the best choice for high-resolution projects where image detail is crucial. It's suitable for film production, commercials, and high-end YouTube content where clarity and sharpness matter. The FX30's 4K recording, oversampled from a 6K readout, produces detailed, sharp visuals even when downscaled.

- **Tips**:
    - Use **XAVC S-I** (All-Intra) for the highest quality and ease of editing, as each frame is individually compressed, which is ideal for complex post-production workflows.
    - Use **XAVC HS** for efficient storage while retaining high image quality, as it uses the H.265 codec with high compression, making it great for long shoots without sacrificing quality.
    - Choose **XAVC S** for balanced quality and file size when you need to preserve storage but don't require the highest bitrate.

2. Full HD (1920 x 1080) Resolution

- **Recording Format**: Available in XAVC S and XAVC S-I formats.

- **Frame Rates**: Up to 120 fps, allowing for high-quality slow-motion.
- **Use Case**: Full HD is suitable for content creators who prioritize file size efficiency without needing 4K quality. It's ideal for social media content, documentary interviews, and when shooting in high frame rates for slow motion.
- **Tips**:
  - Use **120 fps in Full HD** for slow-motion scenes to add drama or highlight specific actions. When slowed down, this footage provides smooth, cinematic motion.
  - Opt for **XAVC S-I** if you plan to work with footage heavily in post-production, as it maintains quality frame by frame, allowing for precise editing without quality loss.
  - For general web content or projects with less intensive post-production needs, use **XAVC S** to save on storage while maintaining a solid level of quality.

3. Proxy Recording (Low-Resolution Files)

- **Recording Format**: The FX30 can simultaneously record a proxy file along with the main 4K or Full HD file.
- **Resolution and Bitrate**: Proxy files are recorded in lower resolution and bitrate, using XAVC HS 1080p.
- **Use Case**: Proxy files are lightweight versions of your footage that make it easier to edit large projects on less powerful computers. These proxies can be swapped with high-quality originals during final rendering to simplify the editing process.
- **Tips**:
  - Enable proxy recording for large, multi-camera projects or if your computer struggles with high-resolution footage.
  - Proxy files are especially useful for remote collaboration; you can share smaller proxy files with editors to streamline the process and reduce data transfer times.

4. External Recording (RAW Output via HDMI)

- **Recording Format**: The FX30 supports 16-bit RAW output through HDMI, compatible with external recorders like the Atomos Ninja V.
- **Resolution and Frame Rate**: 4K RAW at 24, 30, and 60 fps.
- **Use Case**: For projects requiring maximum flexibility in colour grading, such as high-end commercials or films, RAW output provides the best quality and editing latitude. RAW files capture uncompressed data directly from the sensor, preserving detail in highlights and shadows and providing full control over colour adjustments in post-production.
- **Tips**:
  - Use RAW recording for projects that require extensive colour grading or when you want the highest possible quality.

- - Keep in mind that RAW files are large, so use this option only when necessary to avoid overwhelming storage and editing systems.
  - Pair the FX30 with a reliable external recorder, such as an Atomos device, to ensure stable RAW recording and simplify the post-production workflow.

5. Bit Depth and Colour Sampling

- **10-bit 4:2:2 Internal Recording**: The FX30 offers 10-bit 4:2:2 colour depth in XAVC S-I and XAVC S formats, allowing for rich colour gradients and more flexible colour grading compared to 8-bit footage. This colour depth is essential for professional-grade footage that requires high-quality colour accuracy, especially in scenes with detailed colour variations, like nature or fashion shoots.
- **8-bit 4:2:0 Recording**: Available in XAVC S format at lower bitrates, 8-bit recording is ideal for web content or simpler projects where high colour accuracy isn't as critical, and file size is a priority.
- **Tips**:
  - Choose **10-bit 4:2:2** for projects that demand high-quality colour grading or where you expect to adjust exposure and colour extensively in post.
  - For faster workflows or content meant for online streaming, **8-bit 4:2:0** will save on storage without a noticeable quality drop for web platforms.

The Sony FX30's range of recording formats and resolutions gives filmmakers control over the quality, file size, and post-production flexibility of their footage. These options make the FX30 adaptable to a variety of projects, from high-end film production to efficient web content creation.

Frame Rates and Slow Motion Capabilities

The Sony FX30 is equipped with advanced frame rate and slow-motion capabilities, making it a powerful tool for filmmakers and content creators. Here's a breakdown of its functionalities.

Frame Rate Options

The FX30 supports various frame rates for recording, allowing users to choose settings that best fit their project requirements:

- **Standard Frame Rates**:
  - **23.98p** (also referred to as 24p)
  - **29.97p** (30p)
  - **59.94p** (60p)

These options are designed to cater to different production standards, with 23.98p being ideal for cinematic projects and 59.94p suitable for high-motion video content.

- **High Frame Rates**:
    - The camera can record in **4K at up to 120 fps**, which is particularly useful for capturing fast-moving subjects with clarity.
    - In **Full HD**, it can achieve frame rates of up to **240 fps**, enabling extremely slow-motion playback.

Slow Motion Capabilities

The FX30's slow-motion capabilities are enhanced by its high frame rate recording options:

- **4K Slow Motion**:
    - When recording at 120 fps in 4K, the FX30 allows for smooth slow-motion playback at five times slower than real-time, providing a dramatic effect in footage.
- **Full HD Slow Motion**:
    - At 240 fps in Full HD, users can achieve an even more pronounced slow-motion effect, making it ideal for action sequences or detailed analysis of fast movements.

Recording Formats and Compression

The FX30 supports various recording formats that affect image quality and editing flexibility:

- **XAVC S-I**: Offers high-quality intra-frame compression, suitable for professional post-production workflows.
- **XAVC HS**: Provides efficient compression while maintaining high image quality, ideal for longer recordings without compromising performance.

Practical Applications

1. **Cinematic Productions**: The ability to shoot at standard frame rates (23.98p) allows filmmakers to create traditional cinematic looks.
2. **Action Sports and Wildlife Filming**: High frame rates (120 fps and 240 fps) enable capturing fast-paced action with stunning detail.
3. **Creative Visual Effects**: Slow-motion capabilities allow for artistic storytelling techniques, enhancing viewer engagement.

The Sony FX30's frame rate versatility and slow-motion capabilities make it a robust choice for both amateur and professional filmmakers. Its ability to record high-quality video at various speeds opens up numerous creative possibilities, ensuring that users can capture their vision with precision and style.

Storage and Media Options

The Sony FX30 offers versatile storage solutions to accommodate its high-performance video capabilities. With dual media slots, users can choose between CFexpress Type A and SD/SDHC/SDXC cards, providing flexibility for various recording needs.

Media Slot Configuration

- **Dual Slots**: The FX30 features two slots that support both CFexpress Type A and SD cards. This allows for simultaneous recording, which can be useful for backup or overflow storage.
- **Card Compatibility**:
  - **CFexpress Type A**: Ideal for high-bitrate recordings and advanced features. These cards are designed for speed and performance, essential for high-resolution video.
  - **SD/SDHC/SDXC Cards**: More common and often more affordable, these cards can still deliver adequate performance, especially when using higher speed classes (V60 or V90).

Recommended Memory Cards

1. **CFexpress Type A Cards**:
   - **Sony TOUGH CFexpress Type A**: Available in capacities such as 80GB, 160GB, 320GB, and 640GB, these cards are built for high-speed data transfer and durability.
   - **ProGrade Digital CFexpress Type A Cobalt**: Known for reliability and performance in demanding recording situations.
2. **SD Cards**:
   - **Lexar SDXC 128GB V90**: Offers high write speeds suitable for 4K recording at high frame rates.
   - **Sony SF-G Tough UHS-II**: Provides robust performance with high read/write speeds, making it suitable for both video and high-resolution photography.

Recording Formats and Bitrates

The FX30 supports various recording formats that dictate the required media specifications:

- **XAVC HS 4K**: Up to 280 Mbps; compatible with CFexpress Type A (VPG200 or higher) or SDXC V60 or higher.
- **XAVC S-I 4K**: Requires higher performance with a maximum bitrate of 600 Mbps; necessitates CFexpress Type A (VPG200 or higher) or SDXC V90 or higher.
- **Slow Motion Recording**: For S&Q mode at high frame rates (240 fps), a CFexpress Type A card is mandatory due to the increased data rate requirements.

Practical Considerations

- **Speed Ratings**: When selecting SD cards, look for V60 or V90 ratings to ensure they can handle the data rates required for 4K video recording.
- **Simultaneous Recording**: Users can record to both card slots simultaneously, but be aware that the write speed will default to the slower card if different types are used together.
- **Metadata Support**: The FX30 records extensive metadata during filming, which can be leveraged in post-production using Sony's Catalyst Browse software.

The storage options available on the Sony FX30 provide filmmakers with the flexibility needed for various shooting scenarios. By utilizing both CFexpress Type A and SD cards, users can optimize their workflow while ensuring they have the necessary speed and capacity to capture high-quality footage.

CHAPTER THREE
DESIGN AND BUILD QUALITY

Body Design and Ergonomics

The Sony Cinema Line FX30 features a compact, lightweight design tailored for versatility and ease of use in handheld, gimbal, or rig setups. Its body design and ergonomic elements allow filmmakers to operate comfortably over long periods, adapt to various shooting styles, and connect essential accessories. Here's a breakdown of the FX30's body design and ergonomic features and tips on how to make the most of them:

1. Compact and Lightweight Build

- **How to Use**: The FX30 is designed to be highly portable and is one of the lightest cinema cameras in its class. Its compact design makes it easy to carry around for on-the-go shoots or travel projects.

- **Tip**: For handheld shooting or when working in tight spaces, the lightweight design reduces fatigue, allowing you to focus on capturing the shot. Its small footprint is also perfect for mounting on gimbals or drones where weight is a concern.

2. Customizable Button Layout

- **How to Use**: The FX30 has a range of customizable buttons, allowing users to assign commonly used functions for quick access, such as white balance, focus magnifier, or audio level control.

- **Tip**: Customize buttons based on your workflow. For instance, assign a button to toggle between frame rates or adjust audio levels if you often change these settings mid-shoot. This reduces time spent navigating menus and helps you keep focus on the subject.

3. Top Handle with Integrated Audio Inputs

- **How to Use**: The FX30 comes with an optional XLR top handle, which provides additional stability and houses XLR audio inputs for professional microphones, allowing for high-quality audio capture without needing a separate audio recorder.

- **Tip**: Use the top handle for handheld shots that require added stability, especially during low-angle shooting. The XLR inputs are ideal for interviews, documentaries, and projects requiring professional audio, ensuring sync with your footage and eliminating the need for an external audio setup.

4. Vari-Angle LCD Touchscreen

- **How to Use**: The FX30's vari-angle LCD allows flexible viewing angles, which is helpful when shooting from challenging perspectives or in tight spaces. The touchscreen interface provides easy access to focus control, settings, and menu navigation.

- **Tip**: Use the vari-angle screen to frame shots from low or high angles, ideal for creative compositions. The touchscreen autofocus control also makes it easy to shift focus quickly by tapping, which is helpful in dynamic scenes.

5. Tally Lights for Recording Status

- **How to Use**: The FX30 has tally lights on the front and back, indicating recording status at a glance. This feature is helpful for confirming that the camera is recording, especially in fast-paced shooting environments or when the camera is positioned at awkward angles.

- **Tip**: Use the tally lights to ensure that you're recording during critical moments, particularly in single-operator or run-and-gun setups. This is a lifesaver when shooting long takes or fast-moving scenes where missing footage could be costly.

6. Multiple Mounting Points

- **How to Use**: The FX30 features multiple 1/4"-20 mounting points across the top and sides of the body, allowing for the secure attachment of accessories like monitors, lights, and microphones without the need for a cage.

- **Tip**: Mount essential accessories like a small monitor or wireless transmitter directly onto the camera body to keep your rig streamlined and balanced. The built-in mounting points save space and eliminate the need for additional cages, making the setup lighter and more compact.

7. Efficient Cooling System

- **How to Use**: Sony integrated a cooling fan and vents into the FX30 to prevent overheating, enabling longer recording times even in high-temperature environments.

- **Tip**: For extended takes, such as event coverage or interviews, the cooling system helps maintain camera performance. This is especially beneficial when recording in 4K or higher frame rates, as these modes tend to generate more heat.

8. Dual SD/CFexpress Type A Card Slots

- **How to Use**: The FX30 has dual card slots that support both SD cards and CFexpress Type A cards, providing flexible options for recording formats and backup solutions.

- **Tip**: Use **CFexpress cards** when recording in high bitrates or RAW formats, as they offer faster write speeds and reduce the risk of dropped frames. Set up dual recording to simultaneously record to both cards for backup, especially for important projects like weddings or live events.

9. Ergonomic Grip Design

- **How to Use**: The FX30's grip is designed to fit comfortably in hand, providing a secure hold during handheld shooting. Its textured surface enhances grip stability, which is essential for steady footage without additional support.

- **Tip**: Use the ergonomic grip for handheld shots, as the comfortable design reduces strain over long periods. The improved grip also aids in stabilization, allowing smoother shots even without a gimbal.

10. Full HDMI Output

- **How to Use**: The FX30 includes a full-size HDMI output, making it easier to connect to external recorders and monitors for professional video output.

- **Tip**: Use the HDMI output for monitoring in real-time or to record externally in high bitrates or RAW, which provides higher-quality footage and allows for additional grading options in post-production.

The Sony FX30's body design and ergonomics make it a powerful and user-friendly cinema camera. Its compact size, customizability, and thoughtful ergonomic features allow filmmakers to adapt to diverse shooting environments with ease, while maintaining comfort and efficiency on set.

Button Layout and Customization

The Sony FX30 features a well-designed button layout that allows for extensive customization, enabling filmmakers to optimize their workflow and access essential settings quickly. Here's a detailed overview of the button layout and how to customize its functionality.

Button Layout Overview

The FX30 includes several key buttons that can be customized according to user preferences:

- **Custom Buttons**: There are six customizable buttons located on the camera body, labeled as Custom Button 1 through Custom Button 6. These buttons can be programmed to access various functions, enhancing shooting efficiency.
- **Function (Fn) Button**: This button brings up a customizable menu that provides quick access to frequently used settings.
- **Control Wheel and Directional Buttons**: The control wheel and directional buttons (up, down, left, right) allow for easy navigation through menus and settings.
- **Record Button**: A dedicated button for starting and stopping video recording is prominently placed for quick access.

Customization Options

Custom Buttons

Each of the six custom buttons can be assigned different functions based on user needs. Here's how to customize them:

1. **Accessing Custom Button Settings**:
    - Navigate to **Menu > Setup > Operation Customize > Movie Custom Key Setting**.
    - Select the button you wish to customize (e.g., Custom Button 1).
2. **Assigning Functions**:
    - Choose from a wide range of functions, such as:
        - ISO adjustments
        - White balance settings
        - Focus magnification
        - Audio level adjustments

- Display toggles (zebra, peaking)
3. **Example Configurations**:
    - **Custom Button 1**: Set to toggle focus magnification for precise manual focusing.
    - **Custom Button 2**: Assigned to adjust monitor brightness for shooting in varying light conditions.
    - **Custom Button 3**: Can be set to change ISO quickly without diving into menus.

Function (Fn) Menu

The Fn menu provides another layer of customization:

- **Accessing the Fn Menu**:
    - Press the Fn button or swipe up on the LCD screen to bring up the menu.
- **Customizing the Fn Menu**:
    - The Fn menu can hold up to twelve settings that are frequently used during shooting.
    - Users can replace default settings with their preferred options for quick access.

My Menu Feature

For deeper menu settings that are not easily accessible, users can utilize the **My Menu** feature:

- **Pinning Settings**:
    - Navigate to any setting in the main menu and select it to pin it in My Menu for easier access later.

Practical Applications

1. **Fast Filmmaking**: By customizing buttons and menus, users can reduce the time spent navigating through complex menus while shooting, allowing for a more fluid filming process.
2. **Adaptability in Different Scenarios**: Filmmakers can tailor their button configurations based on specific projects or environments, ensuring they have immediate access to critical functions.
3. **User-Friendly Experience**: The ability to customize enhances the overall user experience, making it easier for both novice and experienced users to operate the camera effectively.

The Sony FX30's button layout and customization options significantly enhance its usability for filmmakers. By strategically assigning functions to custom buttons and utilizing the Fn menu and My Menu features, users can streamline their workflow and focus more on creativity rather than navigating menus during critical moments of shooting.

Port Configuration (Audio, HDMI, USB, etc.)

The Sony FX30 is equipped with a comprehensive set of ports that enhance its functionality for audio, video output, and data transfer, making it suitable for professional filmmaking. Here's an overview of its port configuration:

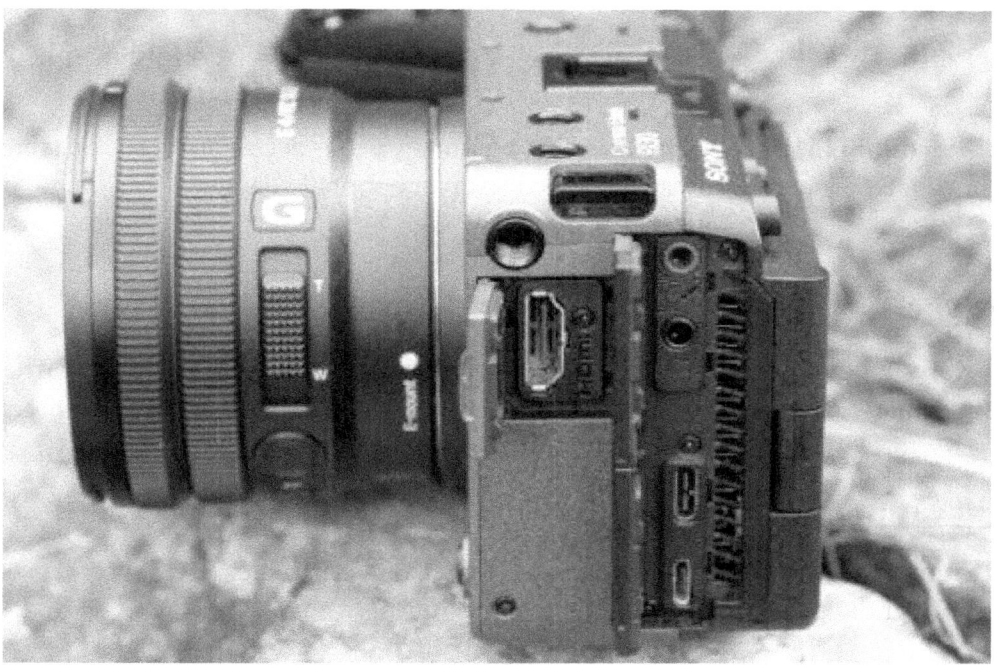

HDMI Output

- **Full-Size HDMI 2.0 Port**: The FX30 features a full-size HDMI output that supports:
    - **Clean 4K Output**: Allows for uncompressed 4K video output up to 60p.
    - **16-bit RAW Video**: Can output RAW video to compatible external recorders, providing high-quality footage for post-production workflows.

This port is essential for connecting to external monitors or recorders, such as the Atomos Ninja V, which can capture high-bitrate recordings directly from the camera.

Audio Inputs and Outputs

- **3.5mm Microphone Input**: This input allows users to connect external microphones for improved audio quality during recording.
- **3.5mm Headphone Output**: Enables real-time monitoring of audio levels during recording, ensuring optimal sound capture.
- **XLR Handle Unit (Optional)**: When using the optional XLR handle unit, the FX30 can support two XLR inputs, allowing for professional-grade audio recording without noise or signal degradation. This is particularly useful for filmmakers who require high-quality sound in their productions.

USB and Multi-Terminal Connections

- **USB-C Port**: This versatile port can be used for:
  - **High-Speed Data Transfer**: Facilitates fast transfer of files to computers or other devices.
  - **Powering the Camera**: Allows users to power the camera during extended shooting sessions.
- **Multi-Terminal (Micro-USB)**: This port supports various accessories, such as remote controls and timecode sync capabilities when used with an optional adapter.

Timecode Sync

- The FX30 supports timecode synchronization through its Multi-Terminal port when connected to a timecode source. This feature is crucial for multi-camera setups where precise timing is necessary for editing.

Additional Features

- **LUT Support**: The camera allows users to apply Look-Up Tables (LUTs) for on-set monitoring and colour grading, enhancing creative control during filming.
- **Metadata Recording**: The FX30 records extensive metadata that can be utilized in post-production, facilitating a smoother editing process.

The port configuration of the Sony FX30 provides filmmakers with robust options for audio and video connectivity, ensuring versatility and high-quality performance. With features like HDMI 2.0 output for RAW video, multiple audio inputs, and USB-C capabilities, the FX30 is well-equipped to meet the demands of professional cinematography.

Weather Sealing and Durability

The Sony Cinema Line FX30 is designed with durability and weather sealing features, making it a dependable choice for filmmakers working in various challenging environments. While it's not completely waterproof, the FX30 has a robust construction that offers substantial protection against dust, moisture, and rough handling. Here's a breakdown of its weather sealing and durability features and tips on how to make the most of them:

1. Weather-Resistant Sealing

- **How to Use**: Sony has incorporated weather sealing around buttons, dials, and port covers to help prevent dust and moisture from entering the camera. This makes the FX30 suitable for shooting in light rain, mist, or dusty environments.
- **Tip**: While the FX30 can handle some exposure to elements, it's advisable to use additional protection, such as a rain cover or waterproof housing, in heavy rain or extremely dusty conditions. Avoid exposing the camera to prolonged moisture to preserve its longevity.

2. Magnesium Alloy Body Construction

- **How to Use**: The FX30's body is made from magnesium alloy, which provides a solid, lightweight structure that is both durable and resistant to bending and impacts. This construction makes the FX30 capable of withstanding the rigors of daily use on set and during travel.

- **Tip**: For projects involving rough handling or movement, like action shots or documentary filming in remote locations, rely on the magnesium alloy build for added durability. Pair it with a rugged case for safe transport and storage between shoots.

3. Dust and Moisture-Resistant Ports and Seals

- **How to Use**: The camera's ports (HDMI, headphone, microphone, USB, etc.) are protected by rubberized covers and are reinforced with additional sealing to reduce the risk of dust and moisture entering sensitive internal areas.

- **Tip**: When shooting outdoors, keep port covers closed when they are not in use to prevent particles from getting inside. For additional security, consider using protective port covers or caps for any open ports during shoots.

4. Reinforced Lens Mount

- **How to Use**: The FX30 features a reinforced lens mount, designed to handle the stress of frequent lens changes and to accommodate heavier, professional-grade lenses without compromising stability.

- **Tip**: For projects requiring frequent lens changes, the reinforced mount provides peace of mind. However, to further protect the mount, avoid applying excessive force when attaching or detaching lenses, especially in dusty or wet conditions.

5. Temperature Management System

- **How to Use**: The FX30 has an integrated cooling fan and a heat-dissipating structure that allow it to operate continuously without overheating, even in warm environments. This is especially important when recording in high resolutions or frame rates, which generate more heat.

- **Tip**: Take advantage of the cooling system for extended recording sessions, such as interviews or live events, where you need continuous shooting without interruptions. However, avoid blocking ventilation points, as this could reduce the camera's cooling efficiency.

6. Shock and Vibration Resistance

- **How to Use**: The FX30's durable build and internal components are designed to absorb minor shocks and vibrations, which is useful when shooting on rough terrains or moving vehicles.

- **Tip**: If shooting in high-vibration environments (e.g., mounted on vehicles), use vibration-dampening accessories for additional protection. This will help maintain image quality and prevent wear on the internal components over time.

7. Operating Temperature Range

- **How to Use**: The FX30 is rated to function effectively in a wide range of temperatures, generally from 0°C to 40°C (32°F to 104°F). This makes it reliable for outdoor shooting in varied climates, whether in colder or warmer regions.

- **Tip**: For extreme cold environments, consider battery performance, as cold can affect battery life. In very hot conditions, periodically check the camera's temperature indicator and let it cool down if necessary to avoid potential overheating.

8. Dust Reduction System for the Sensor

- **How to Use**: The FX30 has a built-in sensor dust reduction system that helps keep the sensor clean, reducing the risk of dust spots appearing on footage. This feature works by vibrating the sensor to shake off particles each time the camera is turned on.

- **Tip**: Regularly activate the dust reduction system, especially when working in dusty or sandy locations. However, it's still essential to handle lens changes carefully and avoid exposing the sensor unnecessarily to open environments.

The Sony FX30's weather sealing and durability features allow it to handle a variety of environments, from urban streets to remote locations, with confidence. For best results, combine these built-in protections with external covers or housings in extreme conditions, and practice careful handling to ensure the camera's long-term performance.

CHAPTER FOUR
USER INTERFACE AND MENU SYSTEM

Menu Navigation and Customization

The Sony Cinema Line FX30 provides a user-friendly and customizable menu system that lets filmmakers set up the camera according to their specific shooting needs. Its menu navigation and customization features are designed to save time, streamline workflows, and make frequently used functions more accessible. Here's an overview of the FX30's menu navigation and customization options, with tips for optimizing them:

1. Intuitive Menu Structure

- **How to Use**: The FX30's menu is divided into clear categories like "Shooting," "Exposure," "Focus," and "Setup," allowing users to find settings quickly.

- **Tip**: Familiarize yourself with each section, especially settings relevant to your workflow. This reduces setup time, and with practice, you'll intuitively know where to find each option.

2. "My Menu" Customization

- **How to Use**: The "My Menu" tab lets you save frequently used settings in one place. You can add options like white balance, frame rate, or audio levels to make them quickly accessible.

- **Tip**: Add high-priority settings to "My Menu" based on the type of shooting you do. For example, if you change frame rates often, having it in "My Menu" saves valuable time.

3. Customizable Function (Fn) Menu

- **How to Use**: The Fn menu, accessible via the touchscreen or "Fn" button, allows you to assign up to 12 shortcuts to commonly used settings like ISO, focus modes, or zebras.

- **Tip**: Arrange shortcuts in the Fn menu that are essential for quick adjustments on set. Having ISO, white balance, and audio levels here can save time in dynamic shooting situations.

4. Touchscreen Interface for Easy Navigation

- **How to Use**: The FX30's touchscreen enables quick navigation through menus and tap-to-focus control. You can use the touchscreen to adjust settings and select options without using physical buttons.

- **Tip**: Use the touchscreen to change settings when shooting handheld or in confined spaces where quick adjustments are needed. Tap-to-focus is especially useful for precise subject tracking.

5. Customizable Buttons for Quick Access

- **How to Use**: The FX30 includes customizable buttons that can be assigned to functions like autofocus, peaking, or exposure compensation. This allows for quick access to frequently used features.

- **Tip**: Assign key functions to buttons you can easily reach, such as focus magnifier or focus area toggle, to avoid interruptions when capturing fast-paced scenes.

6. Control Dials Customization

- **How to Use**: The FX30's front and rear control dials can be assigned to control settings like shutter speed, aperture, or ISO, depending on your shooting mode.

- **Tip**: Assign commonly adjusted settings to the control dials based on your preferences. For example, use one dial for ISO and the other for shutter speed, so you can adjust exposure quickly without entering the menu.

7. "My Dial" Customization

- **How to Use**: The "My Dial" feature lets you assign secondary functions to the control dials, allowing you to switch between primary and secondary settings easily.

- **Tip**: Set up "My Dial" for less frequently adjusted settings, such as white balance or exposure compensation. This feature is useful for rapid switching between different dial functions.

8. Custom Shooting Modes

- **How to Use**: The FX30 lets you save entire shooting configurations, including settings like frame rate, resolution, and picture profile, into custom shooting modes.

- **Tip**: Save different setups for various scenes or lighting conditions (e.g., one for high-speed action and another for low-light shooting). This allows you to switch between configurations quickly without re-entering individual settings.

9. Focus Area and AF Tracking Sensitivity

- **How to Use**: The FX30 offers various focus area options and customizable AF tracking sensitivity to match your shooting style and subject movement.

- **Tip**: Use wide-area autofocus for unpredictable subjects and narrow or zone focus for more control. Adjust tracking sensitivity based on how quickly your subject moves in the frame.

10. LUT Display and Monitor Customization

- **How to Use**: The FX30 allows users to load and display custom LUTs (Look-Up Tables) on the screen to preview colour grading in real-time while filming.

- **Tip**: Load a LUT that aligns with your project's colour grade, especially if you're filming in S-Log3. This gives you a better idea of the final look and helps with exposure and composition.

The Sony FX30's menu navigation and customization options empower you to configure the camera to your specific needs, creating a seamless and efficient shooting experience. By tailoring these settings, you can keep your attention on the creative process and respond quickly to changes on set.

Touchscreen and Control Dial Usage

The Sony Cinema Line FX30 features an intuitive touchscreen and customizable control dials, which streamline camera operation and enhance workflow efficiency. Here's an overview of these features with guidance on how to leverage them effectively:

1. Touchscreen Interface

- **How to Use**: The FX30's touchscreen enables you to navigate menus, adjust settings, and control focus simply by tapping. This functionality is especially helpful in fast-paced or handheld shooting scenarios where quick adjustments are needed.

- **Applications**:
    - **Quick Menu Navigation**: Use the touchscreen to navigate settings quickly by tapping directly on menu items. This speeds up access to frequently used options, such as ISO, white balance, and exposure compensation.
    - **Tap-to-Focus**: With the FX30's touchscreen, you can select your focus point by tapping on your subject on the display. This feature is particularly useful for scenes with dynamic subjects or when you need precise focus adjustments.
    - **Playback and Review**: When reviewing footage, the touchscreen allows you to swipe through images or video clips, zoom in by pinching, and quickly evaluate shots for focus and composition.

- **Tips**:
    - **Use in Tight Spaces**: When handheld shooting or working in cramped environments, the touchscreen is easier to use than physical buttons.
    - **Focus Transitions**: Tap-to-focus is ideal for scenes where you need smooth, controlled focus transitions between subjects, such as interviews or product shots.

2. Control Dial Customization

- **How to Use**: The FX30 includes front and rear control dials that can be customized for easy access to key settings like aperture, shutter speed, ISO, or exposure compensation. This customization gives you faster, direct control over exposure settings, making adjustments easier while you're filming.

- **Applications**:
    - **Exposure Control**: Assign frequently adjusted settings, such as ISO, aperture, or shutter speed, to the front and rear dials. This setup allows you to make exposure changes on the fly without entering the menu.
    - **Focus and Zoom Adjustments**: When using manual focus or zoom lenses, you can set one of the control dials to manage focus or zoom control, allowing more nuanced adjustments.

- **Tips**:

- o **Use for Quick Exposure Adjustments**: When shooting in Manual mode, assign aperture to one dial and shutter speed to the other. This way, you can balance exposure quickly without navigating menus.
- o **Switch to "My Dial" Functions**: Use the "My Dial" customization to assign secondary functions (such as white balance or frame rate) to the dials. This is helpful for shifting between settings that aren't needed as frequently but are still important.

3. "My Dial" Customization Feature

- **How to Use**: The "My Dial" feature provides an extra layer of customization for the control dials, enabling you to toggle between primary and secondary functions quickly.

- **Applications**:
  - o **Flexible Adjustments**: With "My Dial," you can assign less frequently used but still essential settings, like white balance or audio levels, to the dials. You can toggle between primary and secondary functions by pressing an assigned button.

- **Tips**:
  - o **Adapt to Changing Conditions**: This flexibility is particularly useful when shooting in varying lighting conditions or when working on diverse scenes within the same project. Switch between "My Dial" functions for swift adjustments.

4. Fn (Function) Menu and Dial Integration

- **How to Use**: The Fn (Function) menu, accessible through the touchscreen or Fn button, allows you to assign up to 12 customizable shortcuts to frequently used settings. You can also use the dials to make fine adjustments to these settings.

- **Applications**:
  - o **Quick Access Shortcuts**: Place key settings like focus mode, frame rate, and audio levels in the Fn menu, then use the dials for quick adjustments without leaving the menu.

- **Tips**:
  - o **Combine Touch and Dial for Speed**: Use the touchscreen to access the Fn menu quickly, then adjust settings with the dials for precision. This combination maximizes speed and control, making the FX30 adaptable to fast-paced filming environments.

5. Dual-Functionality for Manual and Automatic Modes

- **How to Use**: The FX30 allows you to switch between manual and automatic control of settings such as focus, ISO, and white balance, making the control dials equally useful in both shooting modes.

- **Applications**:
  - o **Adapt for Dynamic Environments**: For shoots that require both manual precision and automatic adjustments (e.g., scenes with shifting lighting), assign exposure

compensation to a dial in Auto mode, allowing you to quickly adjust brightness without changing the exposure settings manually.

- **Tips**:
  - **Practice with Dual Modes**: Test the camera in both manual and auto modes to understand how the control dials respond, ensuring you're prepared to adjust settings effectively in diverse shooting scenarios.

The Sony FX30's touchscreen and control dials offer extensive customization, allowing for fluid operation and greater creative control. By configuring these features to match your workflow, you can make quick adjustments without interrupting your shooting process, enhancing both efficiency and shooting precision.

Quick Access Settings for Filmmakers

The Sony Cinema Line FX30 is packed with customizable settings designed to make filmmaking smoother and more efficient. Setting up quick access shortcuts and custom controls can dramatically speed up your workflow, helping you keep up with the demands of dynamic shoots. Here are some essential quick access settings and tips on configuring them for maximum efficiency:

1. Customizable Fn (Function) Menu

- **How to Use**: The FX30's Fn menu lets you add up to 12 shortcuts to frequently used settings. You can access it directly through the touchscreen or by pressing the Fn button.
- **Essential Settings for Fn Menu**:
  - **Frame Rate**: Quickly change frame rates to switch between slow motion and standard speed.
  - **ISO**: Fast access to ISO control for exposure adjustments in changing light conditions.
  - **White Balance**: Adjust white balance on the fly to maintain colour accuracy in different lighting.
  - **Audio Levels**: Monitor and control audio levels directly without diving into the full menu.
  - **Focus Mode and Area**: Switch between autofocus, manual focus, and different focus areas (e.g., wide, spot) based on the subject.
- **Tip**: Arrange these settings in order of importance so they're easy to find under pressure. If you're working in changing environments, place frame rate, ISO, and white balance at the top of your Fn menu for quick adjustments.

2. Custom Buttons for Quick Action

- **How to Use**: The FX30 includes multiple customizable buttons that can be assigned to frequently used functions, giving you one-touch access to critical settings.

- **Suggested Button Assignments**:
    - **Focus Magnifier**: For precise focus, assign a button to zoom in on your subject for manual focus confirmation.
    - **Peaking Level**: Quickly toggle focus peaking on and off to highlight in-focus areas in manual focus mode.
    - **Zebra Display**: Enable or disable zebras to check exposure in high-contrast scenes.
    - **ND Filter (if using an external one)**: If using a variable ND filter attachment, assign an ND toggle for quick adjustments.
    - **Eye Autofocus**: Map Eye AF to a button for instant access when filming subjects up close.
- **Tip**: Place essential functions on buttons within easy reach, like near the grip or thumb rest, so you can make changes without taking your eye off the scene.

3. "My Menu" for High-Priority Settings

- **How to Use**: The "My Menu" feature allows you to collect your most-used settings in a custom menu tab. This feature saves time, especially for settings that might not fit in the Fn menu.
- **Suggested Settings for "My Menu"**:
    - **Picture Profile**: Quickly switch between different colour profiles (e.g., S-Log3, S-Cinetone) depending on the look you want.
    - **S&Q (Slow & Quick) Mode Settings**: Configure frame rate and resolution for slow-motion or time-lapse without navigating the regular menu.
    - **LUT Display**: Enable or disable your custom LUT preview to see the graded look.
    - **SteadyShot Settings**: Adjust SteadyShot modes based on whether you're shooting handheld, on a tripod, or on a gimbal.
- **Tip**: Use "My Menu" for advanced or infrequently adjusted settings that are crucial but don't require constant tweaking.

4. Control Dials for Exposure and Focus Adjustments

- **How to Use**: The FX30's front and rear dials can be customized to control key exposure settings like ISO, aperture, and shutter speed.
- **Ideal Assignments**:
    - **Aperture Control**: Assign aperture to the front dial to adjust depth of field quickly.
    - **Shutter Speed**: Use the rear dial for quick shutter speed adjustments to control motion blur.
    - **ISO**: If shooting in varied lighting, set one of the dials to control ISO for quick exposure balancing.

- **Tip**: In manual mode, setting the dials to control all three components of the exposure triangle (ISO, shutter speed, and aperture) makes on-the-fly adjustments faster and more intuitive.

5. Focus Control Settings

- **How to Use**: The FX30 offers customizable autofocus and manual focus settings, accessible via the Fn menu or custom buttons for faster toggling.

- **Suggested Settings**:
    - **AF Transition Speed**: Control the speed at which focus changes between subjects, which is useful for dramatic or smooth transitions.
    - **AF Subject Shift Sensitivity**: Adjust the camera's sensitivity to switching focus between moving subjects.
    - **Manual Focus Assist**: Enable peaking or focus magnification for precise manual adjustments.

- **Tip**: For scenes that require varied focus transitions, such as interviews or action shots, make sure AF settings are easily accessible to adjust sensitivity and speed as needed.

6. S&Q (Slow & Quick) Mode Toggle

- **How to Use**: The FX30's S&Q mode allows filmmakers to record in high frame rates for slow-motion or lower frame rates for time-lapse, accessible from the mode dial or a shortcut button.

- **Tip**: Pre-configure your preferred frame rates and resolutions in S&Q mode, then assign a button to switch in and out of this mode quickly. This is especially useful for capturing action sequences or adding dramatic slow-motion effects.

7. Picture Profile Shortcuts

- **How to Use**: If you switch between different colour profiles for different scenes (e.g., S-Log3 for grading flexibility, S-Cinetone for a filmic look), you can set picture profiles in "My Menu" or assign them to a custom button for quick access.

- **Tip**: Store your most-used profiles in easily accessible locations to speed up workflow and maintain consistency across shots. This is especially helpful for multi-camera setups that require matching profiles.

8. LUT Preview Toggle

- **How to Use**: If you're shooting in S-Log3 or other flat profiles, the FX30 allows you to load and toggle a custom LUT (Look-Up Table) for preview. This feature helps visualize the final graded look while shooting.

- **Tip**: Assign a button to toggle the LUT preview on and off. This feature allows you to switch between the flat profile for exposure checks and the LUT view to see how the footage will look after colour grading.

9. SteadyShot and Image Stabilization Settings

- **How to Use**: The FX30 offers multiple SteadyShot stabilization modes, which you can adjust based on shooting conditions.

- **Tip**: Assign SteadyShot options to the Fn menu or "My Menu" to switch between standard, active, or off modes quickly, depending on whether you're using handheld, gimbal, or tripod setups.

10. Histogram and Exposure Settings

- **How to Use**: The histogram can be enabled to monitor exposure levels in real-time, which is invaluable for maintaining optimal exposure, especially in high-contrast scenes.
- **Tip**: Assign a custom button to turn the histogram on and off. This allows you to check exposure during setup and hide it during recording to keep your display uncluttered.

By leveraging the FX30's quick access settings, you can create a customized setup that caters specifically to your filming style. Quick access to essential settings like exposure controls, picture profiles, and focus adjustments will help you capture better shots while maintaining a smooth, uninterrupted workflow.

CHAPTER FIVE
RECORDING MODES AND OPTIONS

Internal Recording Formats and Codecs

The Sony Cinema Line FX30 offers a variety of internal recording formats and codecs that cater to the diverse needs of filmmakers, ensuring high-quality video capture suitable for professional production environments. Here's a detailed overview of these formats and codecs, along with guidance on how they can be used effectively:

1. Recording Formats

The FX30 supports several recording formats, providing flexibility in managing file sizes and quality:

- **XAVC-I (Intra-Frame)**:
    - **Description**: This format records every frame as a complete image, resulting in higher image quality and easier editing due to less compression.
    - **Use Cases**: Ideal for high-budget productions, commercials, or any project requiring extensive post-production work, as it offers the best quality at the cost of larger file sizes.

- **XAVC-L (Long GOP)**:
    - **Description**: This format uses Long Group of Pictures (GOP) compression, capturing key frames and predicting the content in between. This results in smaller file sizes compared to XAVC-I while maintaining good quality.
    - **Use Cases**: Suitable for projects with moderate storage requirements, such as documentaries, corporate videos, and live events where quick turnaround is essential.

- **XAVC S**:
    - **Description**: A consumer-oriented variant of XAVC, XAVC S supports 4K and HD recording with efficient compression. It is particularly optimized for delivering high-quality footage without overwhelming storage.
    - **Use Cases**: Great for independent filmmakers, online content creators, and enthusiasts who require high-quality video without extensive storage needs.

2. Codecs

The FX30 supports multiple codecs, ensuring versatility for different production requirements:

- **10-bit 4:2:2**:
    - **Description**: This codec provides a high level of colour fidelity and detail, capturing a wider range of colours and tonal variations. The 10-bit depth allows for smoother gradients and better colour grading flexibility in post-production.
    - **Use Cases**: Recommended for projects requiring extensive colour correction and grading, such as feature films, music videos, and high-end commercials.

- **8-bit 4:2:0**:
    - **Description**: A more common codec that sacrifices some colour depth but offers sufficient quality for many applications. While it has limitations in post-production colour correction, it produces smaller file sizes.
    - **Use Cases**: Suitable for social media content, vlogs, and projects where fast processing and storage management are priorities.

3. Resolutions and Frame Rates

The FX30 supports various resolutions and frame rates across its formats:

- **4K (3840 x 2160)**:
    - **Frame Rates**: Options include 24p, 30p, 60p, and high frame rates for slow-motion capture (up to 120p).
    - **Use Cases**: 4K recording is standard for high-end productions, allowing for crisp detail and large cropping flexibility in post-production.
- **Full HD (1920 x 1080)**:
    - **Frame Rates**: 24p, 30p, 60p, and options for high frame rates (up to 240p).
    - **Use Cases**: Full HD is suitable for online content, educational videos, and broadcast television.

4. Dual Slot Recording

The FX30 features dual memory card slots, allowing for various recording configurations:

- **Simultaneous Recording**: Record the same footage to both cards for redundancy, ensuring no loss of data during important shoots.
- **Relay Recording**: Automatically switch to the second card when the first is full, extending recording time without interruption.
- **Proxy Recording**: Create lower-resolution proxy files alongside high-resolution footage for easier editing and quicker file handling in post-production.

5. Recording Time and File Management

- **File Sizes**: The choice of recording format and codec affects file sizes. For example, XAVC-I will generate larger files than XAVC-L or XAVC S. It's essential to have sufficient storage based on your shooting duration and selected format.
- **File Management Tips**:
    - Always use high-speed SD cards rated for the required write speeds to prevent dropped frames.
    - Plan for backup storage solutions to manage large file sizes efficiently, especially for longer shoots or multi-day productions.

The Sony Cinema Line FX30 offers a versatile range of internal recording formats and codecs tailored for professional filmmakers. By understanding the capabilities and applications of these formats, you can choose the right settings based on your project requirements, whether it's for high-quality cinematic productions or efficient online content creation. This flexibility ensures that you maintain the highest possible image quality while effectively managing storage and workflow.

External Recording Options (RAW, ProRes)

The Sony Cinema Line FX30 provides filmmakers with several external recording options that expand its capabilities significantly, especially for those seeking the highest quality footage for post-production. Below is an overview of external recording options, focusing on RAW and ProRes formats, along with guidance on their usage:

1. External RAW Recording

The FX30 supports external RAW recording via HDMI, allowing filmmakers to capture uncompressed or lightly compressed video directly to an external recorder. This option enhances the camera's versatility and quality, especially for high-end productions.

- **Supported Formats**:
    - **16-bit RAW**: The FX30 can output 16-bit RAW video via HDMI, which preserves a vast amount of colour and tonal information. This format is ideal for extensive colour grading and visual effects in post-production.
- **External Recorders**:
    - To record RAW, you will need a compatible external recorder, such as:
        - **Atomos Ninja V/V+**: Supports ProRes RAW recording and provides an intuitive interface for monitoring and playback.
        - **Blackmagic Video Assist 12G**: Offers both ProRes and RAW recording capabilities and features built-in monitoring tools.
- **Use Cases**:
    - Ideal for feature films, commercials, and projects requiring the highest image fidelity. RAW recording is essential for visual effects-heavy content where precise colour grading is critical.

2. ProRes Recording

ProRes is a widely used codec in professional video production, known for its excellent balance of image quality and manageable file sizes. The FX30 can record ProRes formats through external recorders when outputting via HDMI.

- **Supported Formats**:
    - **ProRes 422**: This is a high-quality codec offering 10-bit colour depth and 4:2:2 chroma subsampling, making it suitable for colour grading and post-production workflows.

- o **ProRes 422 LT**: A more storage-efficient version, suitable for projects where file size is a concern but still maintaining good quality.
- o **ProRes 422 HQ**: Higher data rates for improved image quality, ideal for high-resolution projects.

- **External Recorders**:
  - o Similar to RAW, devices like the **Atomos Ninja V/V+** and **Blackmagic Video Assist 12G** can record ProRes formats when connected to the FX30. These recorders typically allow you to select the desired ProRes variant.

- **Use Cases**:
  - o ProRes recording is excellent for television production, corporate videos, and documentaries where high-quality footage is needed without the extensive storage demands of RAW formats. It is also beneficial for workflows that prioritize quick editing and rendering times.

3. Workflow Considerations

- **Setup**: Ensure you have a high-quality HDMI cable and a compatible external recorder. Set the FX30 to output the desired format (e.g., RAW or ProRes) via the HDMI settings in the camera menu.
- **Monitoring**: External recorders often provide enhanced monitoring options, including waveform monitors, histograms, and LUT previews, which are invaluable for achieving correct exposure and colour grading.
- **Post-Production**: When using RAW, be prepared for more intensive post-production workflows, as RAW files require processing and colour grading. For ProRes, the files are easier to work with in most NLEs (Non-Linear Editing systems), providing a balance of quality and efficiency.
- **Storage Management**: Both RAW and ProRes formats can consume significant amounts of storage. It's essential to plan your storage solutions accordingly, ensuring you have enough capacity and backup options for your recordings.

4. Advantages of External Recording

- **Improved Image Quality**: External RAW and ProRes recording can provide superior image quality over the internal codecs, especially for high-resolution and high-bitrate recordings.
- **Greater Post-Production Flexibility**: RAW formats allow for extensive colour grading options, while ProRes offers a balance of quality and processing efficiency.
- **Extended Recording Time**: Depending on the external recorder, you may have the option to record to larger capacity storage media, enabling longer recording durations without interruption.

The Sony Cinema Line FX30's ability to output external RAW and ProRes recording options significantly enhances its functionality, making it an excellent choice for filmmakers aiming for high-quality production standards. By utilizing external recorders, you can take full advantage of these formats to achieve professional results while maintaining flexibility in your workflows. Whether you choose RAW for its maximum image fidelity or ProRes for its efficient processing, the FX30 can adapt to a wide range of production needs.

Proxy Recording and Dual Recording Options

The Sony Cinema Line FX30 provides filmmakers with powerful proxy recording and dual recording options, enhancing workflow efficiency and flexibility during production. Here's an overview of these features, their benefits, and practical usage:

1. Proxy Recording

Proxy recording allows you to capture lower-resolution versions of your video footage simultaneously with high-resolution files. This is particularly useful for streamlining post-production processes, especially when working with high-bitrate formats that demand significant storage and processing power.

Key Features:

- **Lower Resolution and Bitrate**: Proxy files are recorded at a lower resolution (such as 720p or 1080p) and a lower bitrate than the primary recording. This significantly reduces file sizes, making them easier to manage and edit.

- **Linking with High-Resolution Files**: The proxy files maintain a link to the original high-resolution footage, allowing for seamless editing in post-production software. Many NLEs (Non-Linear Editing systems) can automatically link proxy files to the original media, facilitating smooth workflows.

- **Easy Editing and Collaboration**: Editing with proxy files reduces the strain on system resources, allowing for smoother playback, especially on less powerful editing machines. This is beneficial for collaborative projects where multiple editors might be working with the same footage.

Use Cases:

- **Documentaries and Event Coverage**: When shooting lengthy events or extensive interviews, proxy recording allows for quick editing and previewing without requiring the full resolution until the final output stage.

- **Multi-Camera Shoots**: In productions with multiple camera angles, proxies make it easier to sync and edit footage from various sources, ensuring a more efficient editing workflow.

2. Dual Recording Options

The FX30 features dual recording capabilities, allowing you to record simultaneously to two memory cards. This functionality is crucial for ensuring data redundancy and managing workflow efficiency.

Key Features:

- **Simultaneous Recording**: The FX30 can be configured to record the same footage to both memory cards. This serves as a safety net, protecting against data loss in case one card fails or becomes corrupted.

- **Relay Recording**: When one memory card fills up, the camera automatically switches to the second card, enabling extended recording times without interruption. This is particularly beneficial for long events or shoots where you cannot stop to change cards.

- **Proxy and High-Resolution Recording**: You can also set the camera to record high-resolution files on one card and proxy files on the other. This setup allows for immediate access to proxy files for editing while preserving the high-resolution footage for final production.

Use Cases:

- **Live Events**: In situations where data loss cannot be tolerated, such as weddings or concerts, dual recording provides an extra layer of security by ensuring you have backup footage.

- **Documentary Filmmaking**: Recording both proxies and high-resolution files allows for immediate editing and review, while still keeping high-quality footage for the final cut.

3. Workflow Considerations

- **Storage Management**: Ensure that both memory cards used for dual recording are of the same speed and capacity to avoid bottlenecks. High-speed cards (UHS-II or faster) are recommended to handle high-bitrate recording without dropped frames.

- **Editing Software Compatibility**: Confirm that your editing software supports proxy workflows and can easily link proxy files to original footage for efficient editing. Popular NLEs like Adobe Premiere Pro and Final Cut Pro X have built-in support for proxy workflows.

- **File Naming and Organization**: Implement a consistent file naming convention and organization system to manage your footage effectively. This will help streamline the editing process, especially when dealing with large volumes of data.

4. Advantages of Proxy and Dual Recording

- **Increased Flexibility**: The ability to record proxies alongside high-resolution footage provides flexibility in editing and speeds up the review process.

- **Enhanced Workflow Efficiency**: Dual recording ensures you never lose critical footage while allowing for easier management of large files during editing.

- **Data Security**: By recording to two cards simultaneously, filmmakers can have peace of mind knowing they have backup footage in case of technical issues.

The Sony Cinema Line FX30 offers robust proxy and dual recording options that significantly enhance the efficiency and reliability of filmmaking workflows. By utilizing these features, filmmakers can streamline their production processes, reduce storage demands, and safeguard against data loss, making the FX30 an excellent choice for both professional and independent projects. Whether capturing high-resolution footage for cinematic releases or managing large volumes of data in documentary filmmaking, these recording options help ensure a smooth and effective workflow.

Creative Picture Profiles (S-Log3, HLG, etc.)

The Sony Cinema Line FX30 offers a variety of creative picture profiles that provide filmmakers with the tools to achieve specific looks and enhance the dynamic range of their footage. Among these profiles, S-Log3 and HLG (Hybrid Log-Gamma) are particularly notable for their flexibility in post-production and their ability to handle high-contrast scenes. Here's an overview of these profiles, their features, and practical applications:

1. S-Log3

S-Log3 is a logarithmic gamma curve that maximizes dynamic range, allowing filmmakers to capture more detail in both highlights and shadows. This profile is designed for post-production workflows that involve significant colour grading.

Key Features:

- **Dynamic Range**: S-Log3 provides an impressive dynamic range of up to 14 stops, making it suitable for capturing high-contrast scenes where detail retention is crucial.

- **Colour Grading Flexibility**: Footage shot in S-Log3 can be extensively graded in post-production, allowing for creative colour manipulation and adjustment of contrast levels without introducing artifacts.

- **Flat Look**: S-Log3 footage has a flat, desaturated appearance, which may require colour grading to achieve the desired look. This flatness is beneficial as it allows for greater manipulation in post-production.

Use Cases:

- **Cinematic Productions**: Ideal for feature films and high-end commercials where precise colour grading is required to achieve a specific artistic vision.

- **Documentaries**: When shooting in diverse lighting conditions, S-Log3 helps capture details across a wide range of exposures.

2. HLG (Hybrid Log-Gamma)

HLG is designed for HDR (High Dynamic Range) content and is compatible with standard dynamic range displays. It allows filmmakers to create HDR content that is viewable on both HDR and SDR monitors without requiring extensive post-production colour grading.

Key Features:

- **HDR Compatibility**: HLG enables the creation of HDR content, providing improved brightness and contrast in images compared to standard dynamic range profiles. This is particularly useful for content intended for streaming platforms and HDR televisions.

- **Ease of Use**: Unlike S-Log3, HLG does not require extensive colour grading to achieve a pleasing image, making it a practical choice for fast-paced production environments.

- **Wide Colour Gamut**: HLG captures a broader range of colours, enhancing the vibrancy of the footage.

Use Cases:

- **Live Events and Broadcast**: HLG is well-suited for live events or broadcasts where quick turnaround is necessary, as it requires less post-processing compared to S-Log3.
- **Documentary Filmmaking**: For documentaries aiming for HDR distribution, HLG provides a straightforward way to achieve high-quality results without the need for extensive grading.

3. Other Creative Picture Profiles

In addition to S-Log3 and HLG, the FX30 includes other picture profiles that filmmakers can utilize for specific needs:

- **Cine1, Cine2, Cine3, and Cine4**: These profiles provide varying levels of contrast and saturation, allowing for different aesthetic choices while retaining good latitude for colour grading.
- **Standard Profiles**: Useful for projects that require a more straightforward look without extensive post-production, these profiles offer a more traditional colour science and contrast.

4. Choosing the Right Profile

The choice between S-Log3, HLG, or other profiles largely depends on the project requirements:

- **Post-Production Flexibility**: Choose S-Log3 if you plan to do extensive colour grading and need the maximum dynamic range.
- **Speed and Efficiency**: Opt for HLG or a standard profile if your workflow prioritizes speed and you need quick results without extensive post-production.
- **Distribution Needs**: If your project is intended for HDR viewing, HLG is the preferred option due to its HDR capabilities.

5. Practical Considerations

- **Exposure and Lighting**: When using S-Log3, it's crucial to expose correctly to avoid noise in the shadows. Use tools like histogram and zebras to ensure proper exposure.
- **LUTs for Monitoring**: Consider applying LUTs (Look-Up Tables) to your monitoring feed to visualize the final look while shooting, especially when using S-Log3.
- **Colour Grading Software**: Familiarize yourself with colour grading software that supports S-Log3 and HLG workflows, such as DaVinci Resolve or Adobe Premiere Pro, to take full advantage of the profiles' capabilities.

The Sony Cinema Line FX30's creative picture profiles, particularly S-Log3 and HLG, offer filmmakers significant control over the visual quality of their projects. By understanding the strengths and appropriate applications of each profile, filmmakers can make informed decisions that enhance their storytelling and production values, resulting in compelling and visually striking content. Whether aiming for cinematic depth or quick HDR delivery, the FX30 equips creators with the tools needed to achieve their vision.

CHAPTER SIX
IMAGE STABILIZATION AND HANDLING

In-Body Image Stabilization (IBIS)

The Sony Cinema Line FX30 features advanced In-Body Image Stabilization (IBIS), a critical technology that enhances shooting stability and reduces the impact of camera shake. This feature is especially beneficial for filmmakers and videographers working in dynamic environments or when shooting handheld. Here's an overview of IBIS, its functionality, advantages, and practical applications:

Overview of In-Body Image Stabilization (IBIS)

IBIS in the FX30 employs sensor-shift stabilization technology, allowing the camera's sensor to move independently to counteract any unwanted movements or vibrations during shooting. This system effectively stabilizes both still images and video recordings.

Key Features:

- **5-Axis Stabilization**: The FX30's IBIS provides stabilization across five axes:
    - **Pitch** (up and down movement)
    - **Yaw** (side to side movement)
    - **Roll** (rotation along the lens axis)
    - **X-axis** (horizontal shift)
    - **Y-axis** (vertical shift)
- **Effective for Various Shooting Situations**: IBIS is effective for handheld shooting, walking shots, and even in low-light conditions where slower shutter speeds are used. It helps maintain smooth footage without the need for additional stabilization equipment.

Advantages of IBIS

- **Enhanced Stability**: IBIS significantly reduces the effects of camera shake, leading to smoother video footage, especially during dynamic movements or when using longer focal lengths.
- **Versatile Shooting Options**: With effective stabilization, filmmakers can explore creative shooting angles and techniques without the worry of introducing instability into the footage.
- **Reduced Need for Gimbals**: While external stabilization devices like gimbals can provide additional stabilization, IBIS allows for stable shots without the added weight and complexity of using a gimbal, making it ideal for lightweight setups.
- **Improved Low-Light Performance**: By allowing for slower shutter speeds without introducing blur, IBIS enhances low-light shooting capabilities, enabling filmmakers to capture clear images even in challenging lighting conditions.

Practical Applications of IBIS

- **Handheld Filming**: For documentary filmmakers or event videographers who need to move quickly, IBIS allows for steady shots without the need for a tripod or stabilizer, making it easier to capture spontaneous moments.

- **Run-and-Gun Shooting**: In fast-paced shooting environments, such as sports or street photography, IBIS provides the stability needed to create compelling footage on the fly.

- **Creative Techniques**: Filmmakers can experiment with techniques like panning and tilting while maintaining stability, allowing for more dynamic and engaging shots.

- **Combining with Optical Stabilization**: When using lenses with Optical SteadyShot (OSS), the combination of IBIS and lens stabilization can result in even greater stability, enhancing the overall performance in challenging shooting conditions.

Workflow Considerations

- **Settings Configuration**: Ensure IBIS is activated in the camera menu when needed. The FX30 allows users to customize stabilization settings to suit specific shooting scenarios.

- **Use of Tripods and Gimbals**: While IBIS is highly effective, for extreme stabilization needs, combining it with a tripod or a gimbal can further enhance stability, especially in long-duration shots or when capturing fast action.

- **Post-Production**: If additional stabilization is required in post-production, consider that IBIS can assist in reducing the amount of correction needed in software, saving time during the editing process.

The In-Body Image Stabilization (IBIS) feature of the Sony Cinema Line FX30 is a powerful tool for filmmakers, enabling them to achieve smooth and stable footage in a variety of shooting conditions. By reducing the impact of camera shake, IBIS allows for greater creative freedom and flexibility, making it an essential feature for both professional and amateur videographers. Whether shooting handheld, in low-light environments, or utilizing dynamic camera movements, the FX30's IBIS technology ensures that filmmakers can capture their vision with clarity and precision.

Digital Stabilization Options

The Sony Cinema Line FX30 offers various digital stabilization options that complement its In-Body Image Stabilization (IBIS) capabilities, providing filmmakers with additional tools to ensure smooth and professional-looking footage. These digital stabilization features are particularly useful for enhancing video quality in challenging shooting conditions or when achieving specific cinematic effects. Here's a detailed overview of the digital stabilization options available on the FX30:

1. Digital Stabilization Overview

Digital stabilization involves software-based corrections applied to the footage after it is captured. This technique helps to minimize shake and vibrations that may not be fully mitigated by IBIS alone. The FX30 incorporates several digital stabilization options, including **Active Mode**, which provides enhanced stabilization for video recordings.

Key Features:

- **Active Mode Stabilization**: This feature is specifically designed for video recording and provides enhanced stabilization by cropping the image slightly to compensate for camera movements. Active Mode can effectively smooth out handheld shots and reduce motion blur.
- **Post-Processing Flexibility**: Digital stabilization can be adjusted in post-production software, allowing filmmakers to fine-tune stabilization effects to match their creative vision.

Advantages of Digital Stabilization

- **Improved Footage Quality**: Digital stabilization can significantly enhance the quality of shaky footage, providing smoother results even in dynamic shooting situations.
- **Complementing IBIS**: While IBIS helps reduce shake during shooting, digital stabilization further refines the footage, particularly in scenarios with significant movement, such as running or rapid pans.
- **User-Friendly Workflow**: The FX30's digital stabilization options are easy to activate and adjust, making them accessible to filmmakers at all skill levels.

Practical Applications of Digital Stabilization

- **Action and Adventure Filming**: In genres where movement is essential, such as action films or adventure documentaries, digital stabilization helps maintain a cinematic feel while allowing for dynamic shots.
- **Sports Coverage**: When filming fast-paced sports events, using digital stabilization can ensure that footage remains smooth and engaging, despite the rapid motion.
- **Run-and-Gun Shooting**: For documentary or event filmmakers who need to capture footage on the fly, digital stabilization offers an additional layer of support for achieving stable shots without elaborate setups.
- **Creative Effects**: Digital stabilization can also be used creatively to achieve specific visual effects, such as simulating a dolly or crane shot in post-production.

Workflow Considerations

- **Understanding Cropping**: Active Mode digital stabilization crops the video slightly, which may affect framing. Filmmakers should be aware of this cropping when composing shots, ensuring that important elements remain within the frame.
- **Balancing Stabilization**: While digital stabilization enhances footage quality, excessive stabilization can lead to artifacts or a "wobbly" effect. It's essential to find the right balance during shooting and editing.
- **Testing and Adjustments**: Experiment with different stabilization settings and evaluate the results in various shooting scenarios to understand how each option affects your footage.

The digital stabilization options available on the Sony Cinema Line FX30, particularly the Active Mode, provide filmmakers with powerful tools for achieving smooth and professional-looking video footage. By complementing the camera's IBIS capabilities, these digital options enhance shooting flexibility and creative expression, allowing filmmakers to capture dynamic scenes with confidence.

Whether shooting action-packed sequences or documentary-style footage, the FX30's digital stabilization features help ensure that your vision is realized with clarity and precision.

Gimbal and Stabilizer Compatibility

The Sony Cinema Line FX30 is designed to be highly compatible with various gimbals and stabilizers, making it an excellent choice for filmmakers seeking to achieve smooth, professional-looking footage. Here's an overview of gimbal and stabilizer compatibility, benefits, and practical applications when using the FX30:

1. Gimbal and Stabilizer Compatibility

The FX30, with its compact and lightweight design, pairs well with a range of gimbals and stabilizers. Here are some key aspects of its compatibility:

- Weight and Size: The FX30 is relatively lightweight (approximately 1.3 kg or 2.87 lbs) and compact, making it suitable for handheld gimbals designed for mirrorless cameras. This weight and size allow for easy mounting and operation on most stabilizers.

- Mounting Options: The FX30 features a standard tripod socket, which is compatible with most gimbals. Additionally, its balanced design facilitates easy mounting and ensures stability during operation.

- Control Compatibility: Many modern gimbals offer features such as remote control and follow focus that can integrate seamlessly with the FX30, enhancing shooting efficiency.

Recommended Gimbals and Stabilizers

Several popular gimbals and stabilizers are particularly well-suited for the FX30:

- DJI Ronin-S / Ronin-SC: Both models provide excellent stabilization for mirrorless cameras like the FX30. The Ronin-SC is especially lightweight and portable, making it a great choice for run-and-gun shooting.

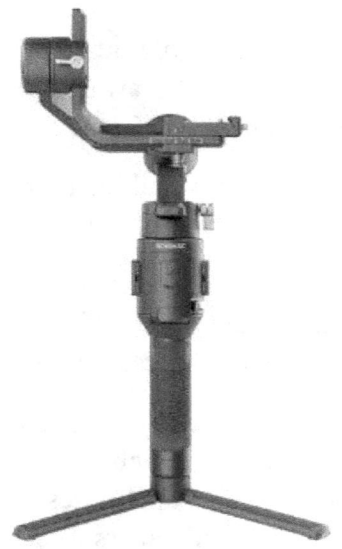

- Zhiyun Crane 2S / Weebill S: These gimbals are known for their smooth performance and advanced stabilization features, making them ideal for cinematic shots with the FX30.

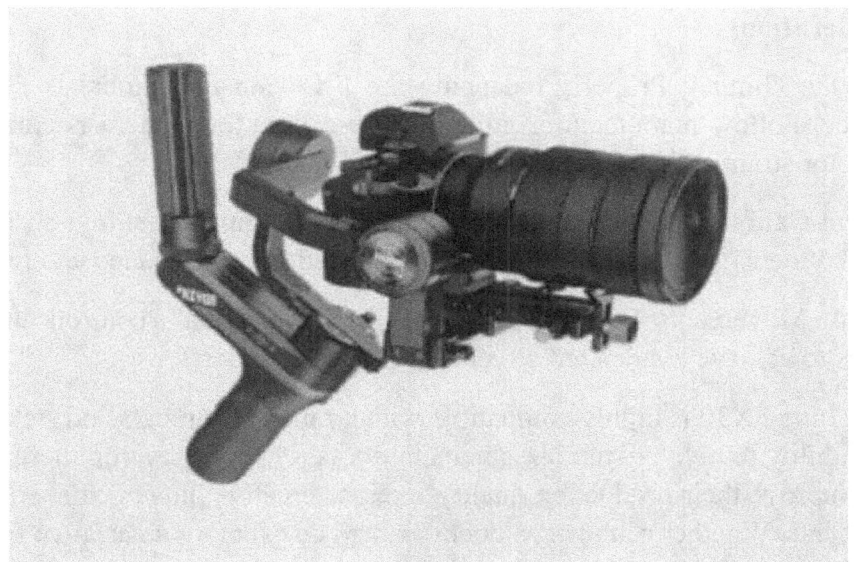

- Moza AirCross 2: A versatile gimbal that can support the FX30, providing stability and advanced features such as object tracking.

- FeiyuTech AK2000C: This gimbal offers a balance of affordability and performance, making it suitable for filmmakers looking to stabilize the FX30 effectively.

Advantages of Using Gimbals and Stabilizers with the FX30

- Enhanced Stability: While the FX30 features built-in IBIS and digital stabilization options, using a gimbal or stabilizer further enhances stability, especially during dynamic movements.

- Cinematic Movements: Gimbals allow filmmakers to execute smooth panning, tilting, and tracking shots that would be difficult to achieve with handheld shooting alone. This capability is crucial for creating engaging visual narratives.

- Increased Control: Using a gimbal provides additional control over camera movements, allowing for precise framing and composition during shots. This is especially useful in narrative filmmaking and commercial projects.

- Reduced Operator Fatigue: Gimbals are designed to balance the camera's weight, which can reduce operator fatigue during long shooting sessions, making it easier to capture extended takes without discomfort.

Practical Applications

- Documentary Filmmaking: In fast-paced documentary settings, a gimbal allows filmmakers to capture smooth, handheld shots while moving through dynamic environments.

- Event Videography: For weddings or live events, using a gimbal ensures stable footage while following action and capturing key moments.

- Action Shots: When filming action sequences, gimbals enable smooth tracking and sweeping movements, enhancing the visual impact of the footage.

- Creative Shots: Gimbals can help achieve creative shots, such as crane-like movements or complex tracking shots, adding production value to projects.

Workflow Considerations

- Balancing the Gimbal: Properly balancing the FX30 on the gimbal is crucial for optimal performance. Follow manufacturer guidelines to ensure the camera is correctly balanced to prevent motor strain and ensure smooth operation.

- Settings and Calibration: Before filming, calibrate the gimbal settings to match the FX30's weight and dimensions, which can enhance stabilization performance and response time.

- Practice with Movements: Familiarize yourself with the gimbal's controls and practice various movements to achieve the desired effects during actual shoots.

The Sony Cinema Line FX30 is highly compatible with a range of gimbals and stabilizers, enhancing its versatility and ability to deliver smooth, cinematic footage. By leveraging these tools, filmmakers can significantly improve their production quality, execute creative movements, and adapt to various shooting environments. Whether capturing a documentary, an event, or a narrative film, using gimbals in conjunction with the FX30 enables filmmakers to realize their creative vision with ease and precision.

CHAPTER SEVEN
POWER AND BATTERY LIFE

Battery Options and Charging

The Sony Cinema Line FX30 offers versatile battery options and charging capabilities, ensuring that filmmakers can rely on extended shooting sessions without interruptions. Here's an overview of the battery options, charging methods, and practical considerations for using the FX30:

1. Battery Options

The FX30 is powered by the **NP-FZ100** battery, which is known for its high capacity and reliability. Here are some key details about the battery:

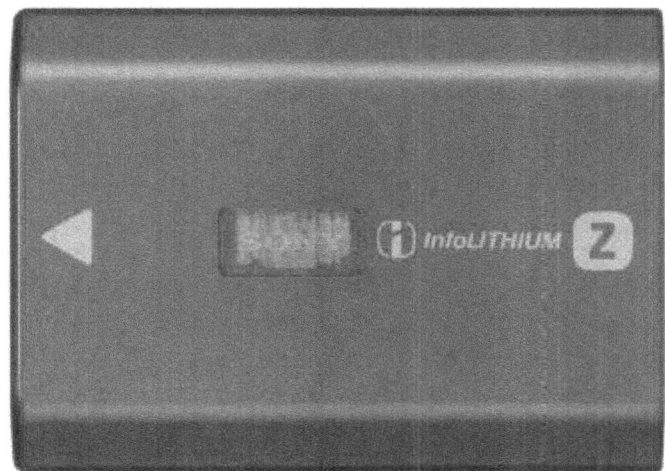

- **Battery Capacity**: The NP-FZ100 has a capacity of approximately **2280 mAh**, providing significant power for extended shooting periods. Under standard shooting conditions, it can deliver around **150 minutes of continuous video recording** at 4K resolution, depending on settings and usage.

- **Performance in Various Conditions**: The battery performs well in both high and low temperatures, making it suitable for a range of shooting environments.

- **Battery Life Indicator**: The FX30 includes a battery life indicator in its menu and display, allowing users to monitor remaining power and plan for recharges accordingly.

2. Charging Options

The FX30 provides several convenient methods for charging the NP-FZ100 battery:

- **AC Adapter Charging**: Users can charge the battery directly in the camera using the AC adapter (AC-PW20), which allows for continuous power while shooting. This is particularly useful for long-duration shoots or when connected to a power source.

- **External Battery Charger**: Sony offers an external battery charger (BC-QZ1) for the NP-FZ100. This allows users to charge additional batteries while using the camera, ensuring they have backup power readily available.

- **USB-C Charging**: The FX30 features a USB-C port that supports charging via USB power banks or wall adapters. This option is ideal for on-the-go charging, making it convenient for filmmakers working in remote locations or during travel.

3. Battery Management Tips

- **Carry Spare Batteries**: Given the demands of video recording, it's advisable to carry multiple NP-FZ100 batteries to ensure uninterrupted shooting, especially during extended sessions or important events.

- **Monitor Battery Usage**: Regularly check the battery status using the camera's display to avoid unexpected shutdowns. The FX30 provides detailed battery information, including remaining percentage and time left.

- **Charge Fully Before Use**: Ensure that batteries are fully charged before heading out to shoot. This helps maximize shooting time and reduces the risk of running out of power during critical moments.

4. Practical Considerations for Filmmakers

- **Battery Life in Different Modes**: Be mindful that different shooting modes (such as 4K recording, high frame rates, or extensive use of autofocus) can affect battery life. Conduct tests to understand how long your battery lasts under specific shooting conditions.

- **Utilize Power Saving Features**: The FX30 includes power-saving settings that can help extend battery life, such as auto power-off after a period of inactivity. Adjust these settings based on your shooting style and requirements.

- **Storing Batteries**: When not in use, store batteries in a cool, dry place and avoid leaving them in extreme temperatures. This helps maintain battery health over time.

The battery options and charging capabilities of the Sony Cinema Line FX30 provide filmmakers with the flexibility and reliability needed for extended shooting sessions. With the NP-FZ100 battery's high capacity, multiple charging methods, and effective battery management practices, users can confidently capture high-quality footage without the constant worry of power depletion. By planning ahead and understanding the camera's power requirements, filmmakers can ensure a smooth shooting experience, maximizing their creative potential on set.

Estimated Recording Times

The Sony Cinema Line FX30 offers varying recording times depending on resolution, frame rate, and file format. Here's a breakdown of estimated recording times based on typical settings and a standard NP-FZ100 battery, along with practical tips for maximizing recording duration:

1. Recording Times by Resolution and Format

4K Recording (3840 x 2160)

- **4K, 24/25/30 fps (XAVC S-I 4K, 10-bit 4:2:2)**:
    - Approx. **70–80 minutes** of continuous recording per fully charged NP-FZ100 battery.

- o **File Size Impact**: 600 Mbps bit rate; consumes significant storage space but provides maximum quality.

- **4K, 24/25/30 fps (XAVC S 4K, 10-bit 4:2:0)**:

  - o Approx. **90–100 minutes** on one battery.
  - o Lower file size than XAVC S-I; suitable for high-quality recording with more manageable storage requirements.

- **4K, 60 fps (XAVC S-I 4K, 10-bit 4:2:2)**:

  - o Approx. **50–60 minutes** per battery.
  - o Higher frame rates consume more power and storage due to increased data rates.

Full HD Recording (1920 x 1080)

- **Full HD, 24/25/30 fps (XAVC S HD, 10-bit 4:2:2)**:

  - o Approx. **120–140 minutes** of recording time per battery.
  - o Suitable for situations where 4K is not required; extended recording time makes it ideal for interviews or long takes.

- **Full HD, 120 fps (XAVC S HD, 10-bit 4:2:2)**:

  - o Approx. **90–100 minutes** per battery.
  - o Slow-motion at high frame rates still provides good recording duration in Full HD mode.

Proxy Recording

- **4K Proxy Recording** (1080p proxies):

  - o Approx. **150 minutes** per battery.
  - o Low-resolution proxies consume minimal battery and storage, making them useful for offline editing and quicker processing in post-production.

2. Factors Affecting Recording Time

Several factors can influence recording duration:

- **Resolution and Bit Rate**: Higher resolutions and bit rates (e.g., 4K, XAVC S-I) consume more battery due to processing demands.

- **Frame Rate**: High frame rates (e.g., 60 fps and above) draw more power than standard frame rates.

- **Environmental Conditions**: Battery life may be reduced in extreme temperatures, especially in cold weather.

- **Camera Settings**: Features like continuous autofocus, IBIS, digital stabilization, and high-brightness screen settings may also shorten recording time.

3. Practical Tips to Maximize Recording Duration

- **Lower Bit Rates for Long Sessions**: Use lower bit rate settings or HD resolution when high-resolution footage isn't essential.

- **Power Saving Settings**: Enable power-saving options, like display auto-off, to conserve battery during breaks.

- **Carry Spare Batteries or Use an AC Adapter**: For extended sessions, having extra batteries or using an AC adapter can ensure uninterrupted recording.

- **External Power Banks**: Use the FX30's USB-C charging port to connect to an external power bank, extending shooting time in the field.

Summary Table of Estimated Recording Times (Per Battery)

Resolution & Format	Frame Rate	Estimated Recording Time
4K (XAVC S-I 4K, 10-bit 4:2:2)	24/25/30 fps	70–80 minutes
4K (XAVC S 4K, 10-bit 4:2:0)	24/25/30 fps	90–100 minutes
4K (XAVC S-I 4K, 10-bit 4:2:2)	60 fps	50–60 minutes
Full HD (XAVC S HD, 10-bit 4:2:2)	24/25/30 fps	120–140 minutes
Full HD (XAVC S HD, 10-bit 4:2:2)	120 fps	90–100 minutes
Proxy Recording (4K proxies at 1080p)	-	150 minutes

These estimated times provide a guideline, helping filmmakers plan and manage power effectively while working with the FX30.

Power-Saving Tips and Tricks

To extend battery life while filming with the Sony Cinema Line FX30, adopting power-saving techniques can be invaluable—especially during long shoots or when extra batteries aren't available. Here are some key tips and tricks to conserve power without compromising too much on functionality:

1. Adjust Power-Saving Settings in the Menu

- **Auto Power Off**: Set the camera to automatically power off after a short period of inactivity. This way, the FX30 will conserve energy if left idle, turning back on quickly when needed.

- **Power Save Start Time**: In the settings, you can adjust the "Power Save Start Time" to a shorter interval, such as 1 minute. This will put the camera to sleep faster, saving battery when you're not recording.

2. Use Display Efficiency Settings

- **Lower Screen Brightness**: Reducing the LCD screen brightness can help conserve battery life. The LCD is a major power drain, so lower brightness when shooting in controlled lighting conditions.

- **Viewfinder-Only Mode**: If you are not relying on the LCD screen, set the camera to use only the electronic viewfinder (EVF). This is more power-efficient than the LCD, particularly when shooting stills or for short bursts of video.

- **Turn Off the Display**: If you're working with an external monitor, turn off the camera's LCD entirely to save power.

3. Minimize Autofocus Usage

- **Limit Continuous Autofocus**: Although continuous autofocus (AF) is beneficial, it consumes a lot of battery. Switch to manual focus when AF isn't essential, or use single AF mode instead of continuous AF.

- **Disable Face/Eye Detection**: If you don't need Face/Eye detection, turn it off. This feature is processor-intensive and can drain the battery faster.

4. Reduce Stabilization Features

- **Limit In-Body Stabilization (IBIS)**: IBIS is helpful for handheld shots but can use extra power. If you're using a gimbal or tripod, turn off IBIS in the menu to save battery.

- **Avoid Digital Stabilization**: Digital stabilization, like Active Mode, requires additional processing power. If physical stabilization tools like tripods or gimbals are available, it's better to use them.

5. Optimize Recording Settings

- **Lower Bit Rate When Possible**: High bit rates require more processing, which can impact battery life. Opt for lower bit rate recording formats, such as XAVC S, instead of XAVC S-I, if your project allows.

- **Reduce Frame Rates**: High frame rates, such as 60 fps or 120 fps, drain more power than standard frame rates like 24 fps or 30 fps. Only use high frame rates when necessary for specific shots.

6. Avoid Using Wireless Features When Unnecessary

- **Disable Wi-Fi and Bluetooth**: Wireless features like Wi-Fi and Bluetooth can be battery-intensive. Turn them off in the menu when not transferring files or using a wireless remote.

- **Use Wired Connections for Remote Control**: If you need remote control functionality, consider using a wired option instead of wireless connections to save power.

7. Use External Power Sources for Extended Shooting

- **Power Bank via USB-C**: The FX30 supports USB-C charging, so connect it to a portable power bank for extended shoots, especially when shooting in remote areas without access to power outlets.
- **AC Adapter for Continuous Power**: If you're shooting in a studio or have access to a power outlet, use the Sony AC adapter to power the camera directly. This removes reliance on battery power entirely.

8. Carry Extra Batteries and Keep Them Warm

- **Bring Multiple Batteries**: Having fully charged spare NP-FZ100 batteries on hand ensures you can swap them when needed. This is particularly useful for long shooting days.
- **Keep Batteries Warm**: In cold weather, battery life can decrease quickly. Keep spare batteries in a warm pocket until you need them, as warmth helps maintain their charge.

9. Monitor Battery Health Regularly

- **Check Battery Health Status**: The FX30 displays battery health status in the settings menu. Replace aging batteries that no longer hold charge efficiently.

10. Quick Battery Refresh

- **Power-Cycle to Refresh**: When you're taking a quick break, turn the camera off completely to save battery. It's faster to restart the camera than to lose power gradually in standby.

Summary of Power-Saving Techniques

Power-Saving Strategy	Action
Auto Power Off	Enable short power-off intervals.
Lower LCD Brightness	Adjust to a minimum brightness setting when possible.
Use Viewfinder	Use the EVF or disable LCD if using an external monitor.
Switch to Manual Focus	Avoid continuous AF when possible.
Disable Face/Eye Detection	Turn off face/eye detection if not needed.
Turn Off IBIS and Digital Stabilization	Disable when using gimbals or tripods.
Opt for Lower Bit Rates and Frame Rates	Record at lower settings when appropriate.
Disable Wi-Fi and Bluetooth	Turn off when not needed for transfers.
Use USB-C Power Banks	Connect to a portable power source for extended shooting.

Power-Saving Strategy	Action
Carry Spare Batteries	Keep extras charged and ready to swap.

By implementing these strategies, you can extend the Sony FX30's battery life significantly, ensuring you get the most out of each shoot.

CHAPTER EIGHT
CONNECTIVITY AND REMOTE CONTROL

Wi-Fi, Bluetooth, and Wired Connectivity

The Sony Cinema Line FX30 provides versatile connectivity options, including Wi-Fi, Bluetooth, and wired connections. These features support remote operation, data transfer, and device pairing, making the camera highly adaptable for filmmakers who require on-the-go control and efficient workflows. Here's a closer look at each connectivity option, along with practical applications.

1. Wi-Fi Connectivity

The FX30's Wi-Fi capabilities allow for wireless file transfers, remote control, and app integration.

- **Wireless File Transfer**: With Wi-Fi, users can transfer files directly from the FX30 to a smartphone, tablet, or computer. This is especially useful for backing up footage on location or quickly sharing clips for preview.
  - **Ideal for**: Quick previews, social media uploads, or low-resolution proxy transfers for editing.
  - **Transfer Formats**: Use Wi-Fi for both high-resolution images and proxy video files to streamline the editing process.
- **Remote Operation via App**: The FX30 can be controlled remotely through Sony's **Imaging Edge Mobile** app, available for iOS and Android devices. This app allows users to start and stop recording, adjust focus, change exposure settings, and preview the shot from their mobile device.
  - **Benefits**: Ideal for single-operator setups or situations where the camera is mounted in hard-to-reach places (e.g., mounted on a jib or crane).
  - **Live View Monitoring**: Provides a real-time preview on the mobile device screen, allowing for remote monitoring when framing shots.
- **Firmware Updates Over Wi-Fi**: Some firmware updates can be downloaded and installed via Wi-Fi, making it easier to keep the camera's software current without connecting to a computer.

2. Bluetooth Connectivity

Bluetooth adds a layer of convenience for pairing devices and controlling basic functions without a constant high-power Wi-Fi connection.

- **Low-Energy Remote Control**: Bluetooth allows for basic control functions using a compatible Bluetooth remote, such as the **Sony RMT-P1BT**. This lets users start and stop recording, focus, and adjust zoom without needing a direct line of sight, as required with infrared remotes.
  - **Benefit**: Bluetooth uses less power than Wi-Fi, so it's ideal for conserving battery during long shoots.

- **Location Tagging**: With Bluetooth, you can pair the FX30 with a smartphone to embed GPS location data into your photos and videos. This feature is useful for documentary filmmaking or any scenario where geographic location tracking is valuable.

- **Automatic Pairing with Mobile App**: Bluetooth also simplifies the process of connecting to the Imaging Edge Mobile app by enabling quick pairing without re-entering credentials or connecting to Wi-Fi.

3. Wired Connectivity

The FX30 includes several wired connection options, providing reliable and fast connections for data transfer, external monitoring, and control.

- **USB-C Port (USB 3.2 Gen 1)**: The FX30's USB-C port supports high-speed data transfer, tethered shooting, and power delivery.
  - **Data Transfer**: Users can quickly transfer footage directly to a computer without relying on SD card readers. This is particularly helpful for transferring large 4K video files.
  - **USB-Powered Operation**: The USB-C port allows the camera to run on external power banks, extending battery life for long shooting sessions.
  - **Tethered Shooting**: With compatible software, users can control the camera and view live feedback directly on a computer, making it suitable for studio shoots.

- **HDMI Output (Full-Size)**: The FX30 has a full-size HDMI port for connecting to external monitors and recorders.
  - **4K External Recording**: The HDMI connection allows for uncompressed 4K output to an external recorder, supporting formats like ProRes RAW.
  - **Live Monitoring**: Connect the FX30 to an external monitor for real-time preview, which is especially helpful in professional filmmaking environments for critical focus and colour monitoring.

- **3.5mm Mic and Headphone Jacks**: Dedicated audio input and output ports support professional audio monitoring.
  - **External Microphone Input**: Plug in an external microphone for better audio quality, a common need in film production.
  - **Headphone Output**: Monitor sound in real-time to ensure audio clarity and consistency.

4. Practical Tips for Using FX30 Connectivity

- **Optimize Wi-Fi Settings**: When using Wi-Fi for transfers or remote control, reduce interference by ensuring that the camera and mobile device are on the same frequency band (2.4GHz or 5GHz) for better stability.

- **Bluetooth for Basic Remote Control**: Use Bluetooth remote control to save battery during shoots that only need start/stop functionality.

- **HDMI with External Recorders**: For higher-quality recordings, pair the FX30 with an external recorder via HDMI, enabling recording in formats like ProRes RAW.
- **Power Delivery Over USB-C**: To ensure continuous shooting, especially during remote shoots or studio setups, connect the FX30 to an external power bank through USB-C to maintain a steady power source.

Summary Table of Connectivity Options

Connectivity Type	Features & Benefits	Use Cases
Wi-Fi	Wireless file transfer, remote control, firmware updates	Remote operation, quick file sharing
Bluetooth	Low-energy remote control, GPS tagging, mobile app pairing	Battery-saving remote control, location tagging
USB-C	High-speed data transfer, tethered shooting, power delivery	Fast file transfer, extended battery life
HDMI	4K external recording, live monitoring	External recording, professional monitoring
3.5mm Jacks	External mic input, real-time audio monitoring	High-quality audio recording and monitoring

These connectivity options give FX30 users the flexibility to work wirelessly for convenience or through wired connections for stability and quality, depending on the shooting needs. This versatility enhances the FX30's appeal for filmmakers who need adaptability across a range of production environments.

Remote Shooting and Monitoring

The Sony Cinema Line FX30 offers robust remote shooting and monitoring capabilities, providing filmmakers with flexibility in setup, control, and previewing footage in real-time. These remote options are ideal for solo creators, complex multi-camera setups, and any scenario where the camera may be positioned in hard-to-reach locations. Here's how to make the most of the FX30's remote shooting and monitoring features.

1. Wireless Remote Shooting with the Imaging Edge Mobile App

Using Sony's Imaging Edge Mobile app, available on iOS and Android, filmmakers can control the FX30 remotely via Wi-Fi. The app offers an intuitive interface for camera control and monitoring.

- **Camera Control**: From the app, users can adjust key camera settings such as aperture, shutter speed, ISO, and white balance, providing flexibility for dynamic shooting environments.
- **Live View Monitoring**: The app displays a real-time preview of the camera's field of view, allowing users to monitor framing, focus, and exposure without needing to be physically near the camera.
- **Touch Focus**: On supported devices, the app allows touch focus control, where users can simply tap on the part of the frame they want to focus on, providing precision focus from a distance.
- **Start/Stop Recording**: Ideal for solo operators or hidden camera setups, the app enables starting and stopping recordings remotely, minimizing camera shake when operating without a dedicated crew.

2. Bluetooth Remote Control Options

For simpler control needs, the FX30 supports Bluetooth-enabled remote control devices, such as the Sony RMT-P1BT remote. This setup allows for basic camera functions without the power demands of Wi-Fi.

- **Start/Stop Recording**: Use Bluetooth remotes for reliable start and stop functionality, ideal for long filming sessions where you want to save battery power.
- **Basic Focus and Zoom Control**: Some remotes support basic zoom and focus adjustments, making them suitable for hands-free control during vlogging or simple setups.
- **Compact and Convenient**: Bluetooth remotes are compact and easy to carry, making them a good choice for travel or minimal setups.

3. Tethered Shooting via USB-C

The FX30's USB-C port enables tethered shooting with a computer, providing stable and continuous control over the camera and access to real-time monitoring software.

- **Sony Imaging Edge Desktop**: For studio or indoor shoots, connect the FX30 to a laptop and use **Imaging Edge Desktop** to control camera settings, view a live feed, and capture stills or start video recording.
- **Tethered Monitoring and Control**: This setup is highly reliable for extended sessions, as it doesn't rely on wireless connectivity and allows for direct power delivery to the camera via USB-C.

4. HDMI Connection for External Monitors and Recorders

For filmmakers who need high-resolution, real-time monitoring, the FX30's full-size HDMI port provides a stable connection to external monitors and recorders.

- **4K Monitoring with Low Latency**: Connect an external monitor via HDMI for a real-time, high-quality view of your shot. This is ideal for critical focusing and exposure adjustments, as HDMI provides the highest-quality signal.

- **External Recording**: HDMI can also connect to external recorders like the Atomos Ninja V, enabling recording in formats like ProRes RAW. This feature provides higher bitrate options and better post-production flexibility.
- **Multi-Camera Setups**: HDMI monitoring is also helpful in multi-camera environments, where an assistant or director needs a clear, uninterrupted view of each camera feed.

5. Application in Different Shooting Scenarios

Here are practical examples of how to use the FX30's remote shooting and monitoring capabilities in specific scenarios:

- **Solo Shooting and Vlogging**: Use the Imaging Edge Mobile app to control the camera from your phone, allowing you to frame the shot, adjust settings, and start/stop recording without assistance.
- **Studio or Controlled Environments**: For tethered shooting, connect the FX30 to a computer for stable control and live feedback, which is helpful in a studio where precision is critical.
- **Action Shots and Difficult Angles**: When mounting the FX30 in hard-to-reach locations (like on a gimbal, crane, or car rig), remote control and monitoring allow for easy adjustments without physically touching the camera.
- **Extended Takes and Battery Management**: With external HDMI monitoring and USB-C power, filmmakers can manage long takes with stable power and high-quality monitoring, ideal for documentary or event filming.

Summary Table of Remote Shooting Options

Remote Method	Features	Ideal Use Cases
Imaging Edge Mobile (Wi-Fi)	Full camera control, live view	Solo shooting, vlogging, hidden cameras
Bluetooth Remote Control	Start/stop, basic focus and zoom	Simple setups, battery conservation
USB-C Tethered Shooting	Direct control, stable power	Studio shoots, tethered sessions
HDMI Monitoring	High-quality output, external recording	Multi-camera setups, high-quality monitoring

With these remote shooting and monitoring options, the FX30 is versatile for a range of filming needs, from solo projects to professional productions. Leveraging these features can improve flexibility on set, streamline workflows, and allow for creative setups that wouldn't be possible with traditional on-camera controls alone.

Compatible Apps and Software

The Sony Cinema Line FX30 is compatible with a range of apps and software designed to enhance its usability, support remote control, and facilitate post-production workflows. These tools provide filmmakers with options for on-set monitoring, remote operation, and seamless integration into editing and colour-grading workflows.

1. Imaging Edge Mobile (iOS and Android)

The **Imaging Edge Mobile** app is Sony's official mobile app for wireless control and remote shooting with the FX30.

- **Remote Shooting and Live View**: Control key camera settings, start/stop recording, and monitor live footage from your smartphone or tablet. This is helpful for solo operators or in situations where the camera is placed in hard-to-reach locations.
- **File Transfer**: Transfer images and videos from the FX30 to a mobile device quickly, even in proxy formats, which is convenient for quick previews or social media sharing.
- **GPS Location Tagging**: Use the app to add location data to your media files, helpful for documentary filmmakers or projects that require geographical data.

2. Imaging Edge Desktop (Windows and macOS)

For users who prefer to work from a computer, **Imaging Edge Desktop** offers a suite of tools for tethered shooting, remote control, and post-processing.

- **Remote Tethered Shooting**: Imaging Edge Desktop allows full control of the FX30 when tethered via USB, supporting precise adjustments and live feedback, ideal for studio setups or controlled environments.
- **Viewer and Edit Tools**: Use the viewer to browse and preview RAW and JPEG images, and access tools for basic edits like colour grading, exposure adjustments, and corrections.
- **Firmware Updates**: Check for and install firmware updates via Imaging Edge Desktop, keeping the FX30's software up to date without requiring direct downloads.

3. Catalyst Browse and Catalyst Prepare (Windows and macOS)

Sony's **Catalyst Browse** and **Catalyst Prepare** software are essential tools for post-production workflows with the FX30, particularly for handling high-resolution footage and stabilizing shots.

- **Catalyst Browse**: A free tool for viewing and organizing footage, Catalyst Browse supports metadata management, basic colour adjustments, and previewing Sony's proprietary footage formats. It's particularly useful for sorting and reviewing clips before transferring them to an editing platform.
- **Catalyst Prepare**: An advanced version that supports batch transcoding, video trimming, and preparation for NLEs (Non-Linear Editors). Catalyst Prepare also offers **gyro-based stabilization** using metadata from the FX30, which can be crucial for smooth, stabilized footage in post.
  - **Gyro Stabilization**: With Catalyst Prepare, users can apply stabilization using the camera's recorded motion data, perfect for handheld shots or run-and-gun filming.

4. Adobe Premiere Pro and Final Cut Pro X Integration

The FX30 produces files compatible with industry-standard NLEs like **Adobe Premiere Pro** and **Final Cut Pro X**, allowing for easy editing and colour grading.

- **Native File Compatibility**: FX30's recording formats (XAVC HS, XAVC S, and XAVC S-I) are directly compatible with Premiere Pro and Final Cut, reducing the need for transcoding.
- **ProRes RAW Workflow**: For users who connect the FX30 to an external recorder (like the Atomos Ninja V), ProRes RAW footage can be imported into Premiere Pro and Final Cut, allowing for higher flexibility in colour grading and post-production.
- **S-Log3 and LUT Support**: These editing programs offer native support for Sony's S-Log3, making it easy to apply LUTs and create custom colour grades, which enhances creative control over the final look of footage.

5. DaVinci Resolve (Windows, macOS, and Linux)

DaVinci Resolve is a popular choice for colour grading and finishing, particularly when working with FX30's high-resolution footage and log profiles.

- **S-Log3 and LUT Management**: Resolve has extensive support for Sony's log profiles, including S-Log3, and offers built-in tools for LUT application, colour grading, and HDR support.
- **RAW Editing and Grading**: When using ProRes RAW files recorded externally, DaVinci Resolve's RAW capabilities provide flexibility in exposure, white balance, and colour correction.
- **Powerful Colour Grading Tools**: Resolve is known for its advanced colour grading tools, allowing filmmakers to fine-tune the aesthetic of their FX30 footage.

6. External Recorders and Monitor Compatibility (e.g., Atomos Ninja V)

The FX30's full-size HDMI port supports output to external recorders, like the **Atomos Ninja V**, which provides additional functionality beyond internal recording.

- **ProRes RAW Recording**: Connect the FX30 to an Atomos Ninja V to record in ProRes RAW, offering higher colour depth and bit rates, ideal for demanding post-production workflows.
- **Real-Time Monitoring**: With an external monitor/recorder, filmmakers can monitor footage in real-time with LUT previews, giving an accurate view of the final graded look on set.

Summary Table of Compatible Apps and Software

App/Software	Platform	Primary Functions	Ideal Use Cases
Imaging Edge Mobile	iOS/Android	Remote control, live view, file transfer	Mobile remote shooting, file transfer on-the-go
Imaging Edge Desktop	Windows/macOS	Tethered shooting, viewer and editing tools	Studio setups, remote control, basic post-processing

App/Software	Platform	Primary Functions	Ideal Use Cases
Catalyst Browse	Windows/macOS	Clip review, basic colour correction, metadata management	Organizing and previewing clips
Catalyst Prepare	Windows/macOS	Batch transcoding, gyro stabilization, clip trimming	Stabilizing footage, prepping for NLEs
Adobe Premiere Pro	Windows/macOS	Full NLE editing, S-Log3, ProRes RAW support	Editing and grading footage
Final Cut Pro X	macOS	NLE editing, S-Log3, ProRes RAW support	Apple-based post-production
DaVinci Resolve	Windows/macOS/Linux	Colour grading, S-Log3, ProRes RAW editing	High-end colour grading and finishing
Atomos Ninja V	HDMI Monitor/Recorder	ProRes RAW recording, real-time monitoring	ProRes RAW recording, on-set monitoring

These apps and software options make the FX30 highly adaptable to different production workflows, from on-set control to comprehensive post-production editing and grading. Filmmakers can select the best tools for each stage of production, maximizing the FX30's capabilities and ensuring a streamlined experience from capture to final output.

CHAPTER NINE
ACCESSORIES AND COMPATIBILITY

Recommended Lenses and Adapters

The Sony Cinema Line FX30 pairs well with a variety of lenses and adapters, allowing filmmakers to capture diverse looks and creative styles. With its E-mount and Super 35 sensor, the FX30 is compatible with a wide range of Sony and third-party lenses, as well as adapters for additional flexibility. Here's a breakdown of recommended lenses and adapters for various shooting needs.

1. Sony E-Mount Lenses

Sony's E-mount lenses are optimized for use with FX30's Super 35 sensor, providing exceptional image quality and seamless autofocus performance. Here are some top recommendations:

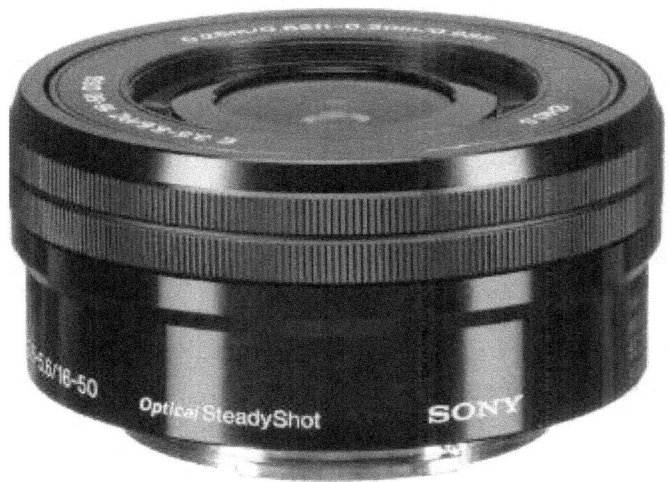

Sony G Master Series (for High-End Cinematic Quality)

The **Sony G Master (GM)** lenses offer superb optics, smooth bokeh, and excellent low-light performance, making them ideal for professional video production.

- **Sony FE 24-70mm f/2.8 GM**: This versatile zoom lens covers a broad focal range, perfect for everything from wide shots to mid-telephoto portraits. Its constant f/2.8 aperture provides consistent exposure and depth of field across the zoom range.

- **Sony FE 70-200mm f/2.8 GM OSS**: Ideal for capturing distant subjects, this telephoto zoom lens provides image stabilization (OSS) for smooth shots. It's great for wildlife, documentary, and event videography.

- **Sony FE 85mm f/1.4 GM**: Known for producing beautiful, creamy bokeh, this lens is perfect for interviews, portraits, and artistic shots with a shallow depth of field.

Sony G Series (for High Quality and Value)

Sony's **G Series** lenses provide excellent optical performance at a slightly lower cost than the GM series, offering a great balance for filmmakers.

- **Sony E 16-55mm f/2.8 G**: This lens is specifically designed for APS-C cameras and offers a versatile focal range, ideal for documentary, travel, and general-purpose filmmaking.
- **Sony FE 20mm f/1.8 G**: A wide-angle prime lens with a fast f/1.8 aperture, ideal for low-light shooting and establishing shots. Its lightweight design is also ideal for gimbal work.

Sony Compact Zoom Lenses (for Portability)

For run-and-gun filmmakers, Sony's compact zoom lenses provide portability without sacrificing quality.

- **Sony E 18-105mm f/4 G OSS**: Covering a wide focal range with optical stabilization, this lens is highly versatile for documentary and handheld shooting.
- **Sony E 10-18mm f/4 OSS**: This ultra-wide-angle lens is ideal for capturing dramatic, immersive scenes or vlogging setups where space is limited.

2. Sigma and Tamron E-Mount Lenses (Affordable and High Quality)

Sigma and Tamron offer cost-effective yet high-quality alternatives, with native E-mount options that work well with the FX30's autofocus system.

- **Sigma 18-50mm f/2.8 DC DN**: Compact and lightweight, this standard zoom is a great choice for handheld and gimbal shooting.
- **Sigma 16mm f/1.4 DC DN**: Known for sharpness and low-light performance, this wide-angle prime is perfect for indoor and low-light shots, as well as for vlogging.
- **Tamron 28-75mm f/2.8 Di III RXD**: A budget-friendly alternative to Sony's 24-70mm, this lens covers a versatile focal range, ideal for travel and documentary work.

3. Adapters for Lens Compatibility

Adapters open up even more possibilities by allowing filmmakers to use lenses from other mounts. Here are some popular adapters compatible with the FX30.

Sony LA-EA5 Adapter (for A-Mount Lenses)

The **Sony LA-EA5** adapter allows the use of Sony's A-mount lenses on E-mount cameras, retaining autofocus capabilities with compatible lenses. This adapter is ideal for Sony users who own A-mount lenses and want to extend their use on the FX30.

Metabones Speed Booster Ultra (for Canon EF Lenses)

Metabones **Speed Booster Ultra** adapters are popular for adapting Canon EF lenses to Sony's E-mount. They offer a 0.71x focal length reduction, which effectively reduces the crop factor, allowing more of the lens's field of view and increased light sensitivity.

- **Canon EF 24-70mm f/2.8L II**: With the Speed Booster, this lens becomes closer to 17-50mm, making it a versatile mid-range zoom with better low-light performance.
- **Canon EF 50mm f/1.2L**: With the Speed Booster, this lens achieves an effective aperture of about f/0.9, providing exceptionally shallow depth of field and low-light capabilities.

Sigma MC-11 (for Canon EF Lenses)

The **Sigma MC-11** is another adapter option for Canon EF lenses, supporting autofocus for a wide range of Sigma and Canon lenses, though some may experience slower autofocus compared to native lenses.

- **Sigma Art Series (e.g., 35mm f/1.4, 50mm f/1.4)**: Sigma's Art series lenses adapted through the MC-11 offer excellent optical quality and fast apertures, ideal for controlled environments and narrative work.

4. Specialty Lenses

For creative shots and unique perspectives, specialty lenses such as macro, anamorphic, and cine lenses are also highly compatible with the FX30.

Macro Lenses

- **Sony FE 90mm f/2.8 Macro G OSS**: Perfect for close-up shots, product videography, and nature filming, this lens offers sharp detail and image stabilization.

Anamorphic Lenses (for Cinematic Look)

Anamorphic lenses create a classic cinematic look with oval bokeh and horizontal lens flares.

- **Sirui 50mm f/1.8 Anamorphic**: Sirui offers budget-friendly anamorphic lenses that produce a 1.33x anamorphic squeeze, which translates to a widescreen 2.35:1 aspect ratio when de-squeezed in post-production.

Cine Lenses (for Manual Focusing Control)

For filmmakers who prefer manual focusing, cine lenses provide smoother focusing and aperture control rings.

- **Rokinon/Samyang Cine DS Series**: These budget-friendly cine lenses come in multiple focal lengths and feature de-clicked apertures, making them ideal for independent filmmakers.

Summary Table of Recommended Lenses and Adapters

Lens/Adapter	Type	Ideal Use Cases
Sony FE 24-70mm f/2.8 GM	Zoom	Versatile workhorse for general cinematography
Sony FE 85mm f/1.4 GM	Prime	Interviews, portraits, shallow depth of field
Sony E 16-55mm f/2.8 G	Zoom (APS-C)	Documentary, run-and-gun, general use
Sigma 18-50mm f/2.8 DC DN	Zoom (APS-C)	Handheld, gimbal shooting
Tamron 28-75mm f/2.8	Zoom	Affordable alternative for mid-range zoom
Metabones Speed Booster Ultra	Adapter (Canon EF)	Full-frame equivalent, light gain

Lens/Adapter	Type	Ideal Use Cases
Sigma MC-11	Adapter (Canon EF)	Adapting Canon EF lenses with good AF
Sirui 50mm f/1.8 Anamorphic	Anamorphic	Cinematic wide shots, horizontal flares
Rokinon Cine DS Series	Cine Lens	Manual focus control for narrative films

With these lenses and adapters, the FX30 can handle a variety of filming scenarios, from high-end productions to independent projects. The range of compatible lenses provides options for achieving different visual styles, allowing filmmakers to make the most of the FX30's Super 35 sensor and dynamic features.

Essential Accessories (Cages, Monitors, etc.)

The Sony Cinema Line FX30 benefits from various accessories that enhance its functionality and usability, especially for filmmakers and content creators working in diverse environments. Here's a list of essential accessories, including cages, monitors, and other tools that maximize the FX30's performance and versatility.

1. Camera Cages

A camera cage provides mounting points for accessories like monitors, microphones, and handles, while protecting the camera body.

- **SmallRig Camera Cage**: The **SmallRig Full Cage** designed for the FX30 (and FX3) is lightweight yet durable. It features multiple 1/4"-20 threaded holes, a NATO rail, cold shoe mounts, and an ARRI-style locating mount for accessories like side handles, top handles, and external monitors.
  - **Add-On Handles**: A SmallRig top handle or NATO side handle can improve handling, especially for handheld shots.
- **Tiltaing Camera Cage**: The **Tilta Full Camera Cage** offers a modular design that includes additional accessories like a base plate, side handles, and top handles for improved ergonomics and mounting options.

2. External Monitors

External monitors enhance visibility and allow for accurate framing and focusing, especially in bright conditions or for high-resolution monitoring.

- **Atomos Ninja V**: The Atomos Ninja V 5-inch monitor doubles as an external recorder, enabling ProRes and ProRes RAW recording. It's compact, offers 1000 nits of brightness, and can capture high-quality 10-bit footage from the FX30's HDMI output.
  - **Benefits for the FX30**: ProRes RAW support, touch-screen controls, and LUT preview options.

- **SmallHD Focus 5 or 7**: These monitors are compact and feature high brightness levels, ideal for outdoor shooting. They come with intuitive touch controls and support custom LUTs, enabling filmmakers to preview the final look of their footage.
- **PortKeys BM5 III**: This 5.5-inch monitor offers 2200 nits of brightness, making it excellent for daylight visibility. It also includes professional tools like waveform monitoring, false colour, and peaking.

3. Microphones

High-quality audio is crucial for professional video production, so adding an external microphone to the FX30 is highly recommended.

- **Rode VideoMic NTG**: This shotgun microphone delivers clear audio and mounts directly onto the camera's cold shoe. It connects via a 3.5mm jack and is ideal for on-camera recording, providing better sound quality than the FX30's built-in microphone.
- **Sony XLR-K3M Adapter**: This XLR adapter allows for the use of professional-grade microphones and connects directly to the FX30's MI (Multi-Interface) shoe, providing up to two XLR inputs. It's ideal for interviews, documentaries, and any work requiring high-quality, balanced audio inputs.
- **Sennheiser MKE 600**: Another shotgun microphone, the MKE 600 is designed for capturing directional sound with excellent clarity, suitable for documentary, narrative, and interview work.

4. Power Solutions

Extended power options ensure the FX30 can handle long shooting sessions without interruptions.

- **Sony NP-FZ100 Batteries**: The FX30 uses Sony's NP-FZ100 batteries, which provide good battery life. Keeping several spares on hand is essential for extended shoots.
- **Anker PowerCore+ 26800 PD**: A high-capacity power bank like this can power the FX30 via its USB-C port, providing an alternative power source for extended shooting sessions when AC power isn't available.
- **Dummy Battery Adapter**: A dummy battery connected to an external power source (like a V-mount battery or DC power adapter) enables continuous power, especially useful for studio setups or long takes.

5. Memory Cards

The FX30 supports **CFexpress Type A** and **SDXC** cards, and high-quality, high-speed cards are crucial for 4K recording.

- **Sony Tough CFexpress Type A Cards**: These cards are rugged and optimized for high-speed recording, essential for 4K XAVC S-I recording and high-bitrate codecs.
- **SanDisk Extreme Pro SDXC UHS-II**: For users not needing the highest recording bitrates, UHS-II SD cards offer reliable performance and ample speed for the FX30's 4K and HD modes.

6. Tripods and Stabilizers

Stabilizing the FX30 is essential for smooth shots, especially in handheld and moving scenarios.

- **Manfrotto Befree Advanced Tripod**: Compact and lightweight, this tripod offers stability and portability, ideal for travel filmmaking.
- **DJI RS 3 Gimbal Stabilizer**: The RS 3 gimbal provides smooth stabilization and supports the FX30's weight with additional accessories. It features quick setup, fine-tuning balance options, and modes like ActiveTrack for dynamic movement.
- **Zhiyun Crane 3S**: For heavier setups, the Crane 3S offers high payload capacity and professional stabilization features, including modular handle options and dual focus control for smooth, cinematic shots.

7. ND Filters

ND filters are essential for controlling exposure in bright conditions and achieving shallow depth of field.

- **PolarPro Quartzline ND Filters**: PolarPro's Quartzline filters are known for their durability and colour accuracy. Options include fixed NDs and variable ND filters, suitable for various lighting conditions and creative needs.
- **Tiffen Variable ND Filter**: Tiffen's variable ND filter allows for quick adjustments without swapping filters, ideal for run-and-gun shooting.

8. Data Management Solutions

Efficient data management ensures quick and reliable storage of footage, which is especially crucial for high-resolution and high-bitrate files.

- **Samsung T7 Portable SSD**: With high-speed transfer rates and compact design, the T7 SSD is ideal for offloading footage on set or for storing data in the field.
- **G-Technology ArmorATD External Hard Drive**: Built for durability, this rugged drive provides secure storage for fieldwork and travel, with shock-resistant casing.

9. Other Useful Accessories

Additional tools can further optimize the FX30's performance and convenience.

- **HDMI Lock Cable Clamp**: To secure HDMI cables during shoots, an HDMI lock clamp is essential, especially when using external monitors or recorders.
- **Lens Cleaning Kit**: Keeping lenses and sensors clean is essential for image quality. A basic kit includes a blower, microfiber cloths, and lens cleaning solution.
- **Screen Protector**: To prevent scratches on the FX30's screen, a tempered glass screen protector is highly recommended, especially for rugged shooting environments.

Summary Table of Essential Accessories

Accessory	Purpose	Recommended Model(s)
Cage	Mounting points and protection	SmallRig Full Cage, Tiltaing Cage
External Monitor	Improved visibility and framing	Atomos Ninja V, SmallHD Focus
Microphone	High-quality audio capture	Rode VideoMic NTG, Sony XLR-K3M
Power Bank	Extended power in the field	Anker PowerCore+ 26800 PD
Memory Card	High-speed storage for 4K video	Sony Tough CFexpress, SanDisk Extreme Pro
Tripod	Stable support for fixed shots	Manfrotto Befree Advanced
Gimbal Stabilizer	Smooth movement and dynamic shots	DJI RS 3, Zhiyun Crane 3S
ND Filter	Exposure control in bright conditions	PolarPro Quartzline, Tiffen Variable ND
Portable SSD	Data storage and transfer	Samsung T7, G-Technology ArmorATD
HDMI Lock Clamp	Secures HDMI cables	SmallRig HDMI Cable Clamp
Lens Cleaning Kit	Lens and sensor maintenance	Generic lens cleaning kit
Screen Protector	Protection for LCD screen	Tempered glass protector

These essential accessories can greatly enhance the FX30's usability, functionality, and overall performance, catering to the diverse demands of filmmaking environments. Together, they provide the tools necessary for both solo shooters and professional film crews to achieve high-quality results in a range of production scenarios.

Power Accessories and Storage Solutions

For filmmakers using the Sony Cinema Line FX30, power accessories and storage solutions are crucial for uninterrupted shooting and managing high-resolution footage. Below is a comprehensive guide to recommended power accessories and storage options that maximize the camera's uptime and ensure efficient data management.

Power Accessories

The FX30 is compatible with various power options to support long shooting sessions, both in the studio and on location.

1. **Batteries**
   - **Sony NP-FZ100 Batteries**: The FX30 uses Sony's NP-FZ100 battery, which provides solid runtime per charge. These are a must-have for primary power, and it's advisable to carry multiple spare batteries for long shoots.

2. **Battery Grips**
   - **Sony VG-C4EM Vertical Grip**: Although primarily designed for the Sony Alpha series, the grip is compatible with cameras using NP-FZ100 batteries. It enables dual battery use, doubling battery life and providing a more comfortable grip for handheld shooting.

3. **USB-C Power Banks**
   - **Anker PowerCore+ 26800 PD**: With a USB-C PD (Power Delivery) feature, this power bank can power the FX30 via its USB-C port, ideal for extended shoots when AC power isn't available.
   - **Omni 20+ Power Bank**: This high-capacity power bank offers multiple output options, including USB-C PD, making it versatile for charging or powering the FX30 in the field.

4. **AC Power Adapters**
   - **Sony AC Adapter AC-PW20**: For studio setups, the AC-PW20 adapter allows the FX30 to run continuously without relying on battery power. It's ideal for long recording sessions or live-streaming scenarios.

5. **Dummy Battery Adapters**
   - **NP-FZ100 Dummy Battery with DC Coupler**: A dummy battery adapter connects to an external power source (like a V-mount battery), providing continuous power for uninterrupted shooting. It's useful for time-lapse, studio setups, and long-take filming.

6. **V-Mount Batteries**
   - **Fxlion Nano One V-Mount Battery**: Compact and lightweight, this V-mount battery can connect to a dummy battery or directly to the FX30 (with a V-mount adapter plate). Ideal for high-power, long-duration filming setups.
   - **Core SWX Powerbase EDGE**: This versatile V-mount battery doubles as a base grip, with multiple outputs (USB, D-Tap), offering extended power for the FX30 and other on-set accessories like monitors and lights.

Storage Solutions

With the FX30's high-bitrate video recording, reliable and fast storage solutions are critical to handle large files and ensure efficient workflow.

1. **Memory Cards**
   - **Sony Tough CFexpress Type A Cards**: The FX30 supports CFexpress Type A cards for faster data transfer rates, ideal for 4K XAVC S-I recording. These cards are rugged, water-resistant, and reliable for high-bitrate recording.

- **SanDisk Extreme Pro SDXC UHS-II**: For projects not requiring the maximum bitrates, UHS-II SD cards offer a balance between cost and performance. These cards support 4K recording and are widely available.

2. External SSDs

- **Samsung T7 Portable SSD**: Compact and reliable, the T7 is great for offloading footage from the FX30. With USB-C connectivity, it provides fast transfer speeds, ideal for on-the-go editing.
- **SanDisk Extreme Pro Portable SSD V2**: Known for its rugged build and high speeds, this SSD is dust and water-resistant, making it a robust option for fieldwork.
- **G-Technology ArmorATD External Hard Drive**: This rugged drive offers durability and reliability with shock resistance, ideal for backing up footage in challenging environments.

3. SSDs for Direct Recording (via External Recorder)

- **Angelbird AtomX SSDmini**: When using the FX30 with an Atomos Ninja V or other external recorders, the AtomX SSDmini is optimized for direct recording of high-bitrate formats like ProRes and ProRes RAW.
- **Sony AtomX SSD**: This SSD is designed for seamless use with Atomos recorders and provides reliable performance for direct recording of high-quality video footage.

4. Multi-Card Readers

- **Sony CFexpress Type A and SD Card Reader**: This dual-slot reader enables quick transfers of CFexpress Type A and SD cards, saving time in post-production.
- **ProGrade Digital CFexpress & SD Dual-Slot Reader**: With a USB 3.2 Gen 2 interface, this reader offers fast transfers and supports both CFexpress and SD cards, ensuring compatibility with the FX30's storage options.

Summary Table of Power Accessories and Storage Solutions

Accessory Type	Recommended Models	Key Benefits
Batteries	Sony NP-FZ100	Long-lasting power for primary use
Battery Grips	Sony VG-C4EM	Dual battery use for extended runtime
USB-C Power Banks	Anker PowerCore+ 26800 PD, Omni 20+	Extended power in remote locations
AC Power Adapter	Sony AC Adapter AC-PW20	Continuous power in studio settings
Dummy Battery Adapters	NP-FZ100 Dummy Battery	Continuous power for studio/long shoots

Accessory Type	Recommended Models	Key Benefits
V-Mount Batteries	Fxlion Nano One, Core SWX Powerbase	High-capacity power for extended shooting
Memory Cards	Sony Tough CFexpress Type A, SanDisk Extreme Pro	Fast storage for high-bitrate video
External SSDs	Samsung T7, SanDisk Extreme Pro	Portable, high-speed data storage
Direct Recording SSDs	Angelbird AtomX SSDmini	Optimized for Atomos recording setups
Multi-Card Readers	Sony CFexpress & SD Reader	Fast card offloading and workflow

These power accessories and storage solutions ensure the Sony Cinema Line FX30 operates smoothly in various shooting conditions, from outdoor locations to controlled studio environments. Carrying multiple power and storage options allows for flexibility, uninterrupted filming, and a streamlined data management process for both on-set review and post-production tasks.

CHAPTER TEN
WORKFLOW AND POST-PRODUCTION

File Transfer and Media Management

The Sony FX30 offers several methods for transferring files and managing media, catering to both professional filmmakers and content creators. Here's an overview of the available options and best practices for efficient file transfer and media management.

1. **Direct USB Transfer**

   - **USB-C Connection**: The FX30 can be connected directly to a computer using a USB-C cable. This allows for high-speed data transfer of images and videos.

     - **Steps**:

       1. Connect the FX30 to your computer using the supplied USB-C cable.
       2. Open **File Explorer** (Windows) or **Finder** (Mac).
       3. Locate the camera in the file directory.
       4. Navigate to the folder containing your media, then copy and paste the files into your desired location on your computer

2. **Using Memory Cards**

   - **SD/CFexpress Type A Cards**: The FX30 features dual slots for CFexpress Type A and SD cards, allowing users to remove the card from the camera and insert it directly into a card reader connected to a computer.

     - **Steps**:

       1. Eject the memory card from the FX30.
       2. Insert it into a compatible card reader connected to your computer.
       3. Access the card through File Explorer or Finder, locate your media, and copy it to your computer.

3. **Smartphone Transfer**

   - **Wireless Transfer**: The FX30 supports transferring images to smartphones via Wi-Fi using Sony's Creators' App.

     - **Steps**:

       1. Pair the camera with your smartphone through Wi-Fi.
       2. On the camera, navigate to **MENU > Network > Connect/Remote Shoot > Select on Cam & Send**.
       3. Choose the images you wish to transfer and follow prompts to complete the transfer

- **File Size Options**: Users can select between different image sizes for transfer (original or reduced size) depending on their needs.

4. **Using Imaging Edge Software**

   - **Sony Imaging Edge**: After transferring files to a computer, users can utilize Sony's Imaging Edge software for organizing, viewing, and editing images.
     - This software allows for metadata management, making it easier for filmmakers to keep track of their footage during post-production

5. **Format Considerations for Editing**

   - When transferring footage for editing, especially on mobile devices like iPhones, it's essential to choose compatible formats:
     - Switching from **10-bit 4:2:2** to **8-bit 4:2:0** in the recording settings can facilitate easier transfers and compatibility with mobile editing applications

The Sony FX30 provides multiple options for file transfer and media management, making it versatile for various workflows. Whether connecting directly via USB-C, using memory cards, or transferring wirelessly to smartphones, users can efficiently manage their footage for editing and sharing. Utilizing software like Sony Imaging Edge further enhances post-production capabilities by allowing detailed organization and editing of captured media.

Colour Grading with Sony's Picture Profiles

Colour grading is a crucial step in the post-production process, especially for footage shot with the Sony FX30, which offers various picture profiles that enhance creative flexibility. This guide outlines how to effectively use these profiles, particularly S-Log3/SGamut3.Cine, for optimal results in colour grading software like DaVinci Resolve.

Understanding Picture Profiles

1. **S-Log3/SGamut3.Cine**:
   - **Purpose**: Designed for maximum dynamic range and flexibility in post-production, S-Log3 captures a flat image that retains detail in shadows and highlights.
   - **Benefits**: It allows for extensive colour grading capabilities, making it ideal for cinematic projects.

2. **Rec.709**:
   - **Purpose**: A standard colour space for HD video, suitable for projects that require less post-processing.
   - **Use Case**: Great for quick turnarounds where minimal grading is needed.

Colour Grading Workflow

1. **Shooting Settings**
   - When using the FX30, shoot in S-Log3/SGamut3.Cine to maximize your grading potential. This setting provides a flat image that can be easily manipulated during colour grading.

2. **Importing Footage into DaVinci Resolve**
   - After shooting, import your S-Log3 footage into DaVinci Resolve. Ensure your project settings match your footage specifications (e.g., frame rate, resolution).

3. **Initial Setup**
   - **Colour Space Transform (CST)**: Apply a CST node to convert S-Log3 to Rec.709 for easier grading.
     - Steps:
       1. Right-click on your clip in the timeline.
       2. Go to **Effects > Colour Space Transform**.
       3. Set the input colour space to **Sony S-Gamut3.Cine** and input gamma to **S-Log3**.
       4. Set output colour space to **Rec.709** and gamma to **Rec.709**.

4. **Basic Corrections**
   - Adjust exposure, contrast, and white balance:
     - Use the **Camera Raw settings** to refine exposure and contrast.
     - Adjust white balance to achieve natural skin tones and accurate colours.

5. **Creative Grading**
   - After establishing a solid base correction:
     - Apply creative LUTs or manually adjust colours using curves and wheels.
     - Focus on enhancing skin tones, adjusting shadows/highlights, and adding stylistic elements (e.g., film grain or bloom effects).

6. **Final Touches**
   - Use tools like noise reduction and sharpening to enhance image quality further.
   - Monitor scopes (waveform, vectorscope) to ensure proper exposure and colour balance throughout your grading process.

Practical Tips

- **Use LUTs Wisely**: While LUTs can speed up the grading process, ensure they complement your footage rather than overpower it.

- **Experiment with Looks**: Try different film emulation presets or create custom looks that suit your project's mood.
- **Regularly Check Scopes**: Keep an eye on your scopes to avoid clipping highlights or crushing shadows.

Colour grading with Sony's picture profiles, particularly S-Log3/SGamut3.Cine on the FX30, allows filmmakers to achieve stunning results by providing a flexible foundation for creative expression in post-production. By following a structured workflow in DaVinci Resolve and leveraging the camera's capabilities, users can enhance their footage significantly and deliver professional-quality videos.

Editing and Post-Production Tips

When working with footage from the Sony FX30, effective editing and post-production techniques can significantly enhance the final output. Here are some key tips based on various resources that focus on color grading, exposure settings, and overall workflow optimization.

1. **Utilizing Picture Profiles for Color Grading**

- **S-Log3/SGamut3.Cine**: This profile is ideal for capturing a wide dynamic range and flexibility in post-production. It allows for extensive color grading options, which is essential for achieving cinematic looks.
  - **Exposure Tips**: When shooting in S-Log3, it's recommended to slightly overexpose your footage to retain detail in shadows while minimizing noise. The base ISOs for S-Log3 are typically **800** and **2500**, which provide the cleanest image quality with minimal noise

2. **Color Grading Workflow in DaVinci Resolve**

- **Importing Footage**: Start by importing your S-Log3 footage into DaVinci Resolve. Set your project settings to match your footage specifications (resolution, frame rate).
- **Color Space Transform (CST)**: Use a CST node to convert S-Log3 to Rec.709 for easier grading. This helps in visualizing how your footage will look after grading.
- **Basic Corrections**:
  - Adjust exposure, contrast, and white balance using the Camera Raw settings to establish a solid base before applying creative grades
  - Monitor scopes (waveform, vectorscope) to ensure proper exposure and color balance throughout the grading process.

3. **Creative Grading Techniques**

- **Use of LUTs**: Incorporate LUTs designed for S-Log3 to speed up the grading process. However, adjust them as needed to ensure they complement your footage rather than overpower it

- **Film Emulation**: Consider using film emulation plugins or presets to achieve specific looks (e.g., Kodak film emulations). Adjust color density and tonal contrast to enhance the overall aesthetic

4. **Enhancing Skin Tones and Color Balance**

- Pay special attention to skin tones during grading. Use targeted adjustments to ensure they appear natural, avoiding overly warm or cool casts that can detract from the overall quality of your footage

- Utilize tools within DaVinci Resolve, such as curves and HSL (Hue, Saturation, Lightness) adjustments, to refine colors selectively.

5. **Final Touches**

- After achieving your desired look, consider adding effects like noise reduction or sharpening to enhance image quality further.

- Apply film grain subtly if desired, but be cautious not to overdo it; a natural look is often more appealing than an overly processed one

6. **Efficient File Management**

- Use Sony's Imaging Edge software for organizing and managing your media files effectively after transferring them from the FX30.

- Maintain a consistent file structure on your storage devices to streamline access during editing sessions.

Editing and post-production with the Sony FX30 can yield stunning results when leveraging its advanced features and following best practices in color grading and workflow management. By utilizing S-Log3 effectively, employing creative grading techniques, and ensuring efficient media management, filmmakers can significantly enhance their projects' visual quality and storytelling impact.

CHAPTER ELEVEN
COMPARISON WITH OTHER CINEMA LINE CAMERAS

FX30 vs FX3: Key Differences

The Sony FX30 and FX3 are both advanced cinema cameras that share many features but differ significantly in key areas. Below is a comparison highlighting their main differences:

1. Sensor Size and Resolution

- **FX30**: Features a **26.1 MP APS-C BSI CMOS sensor**. This smaller sensor offers a **1.5x crop factor**, which affects the field of view when using full-frame lenses.

- **FX3**: Equipped with a **12.1 MP Full-Frame BSI CMOS sensor**, providing a wider field of view and better performance in low-light conditions due to larger photosites.

2. ISO Range

- **FX30**: Normal ISO range of **100 to 32,000**, with an extended range up to **102,400**. Dual base ISO at **800 and 2,500**.

- **FX3**: Wider normal ISO range of **80 to 102,400**, extending to **50 - 409,600**. Dual base ISO at **2,500 and 4,000**, allowing for cleaner images in low-light situations.

3. Autofocus System

- **FX30**: Contains **495 phase-detection points** for autofocus.

- **FX3**: Offers a more advanced system with **627 phase-detection points**, enhancing focus accuracy and speed, especially in challenging lighting conditions.

4. LCD Screen

- **FX30**: Boasts a higher resolution **3-inch vari-angle LCD screen** with **2.36 million dots**, providing better clarity for monitoring.

- **FX3**: Features the same size screen but with a lower resolution of **1.44 million dots**.

5. Continuous Shooting Capability

- **FX30**: Limited to continuous shooting at **1 fps**, making it less suitable for high-speed photography.

- **FX3**: Supports continuous shooting at up to **10 fps**, providing greater flexibility for capturing fast-moving subjects.

6. Weight and Build

- **FX30**: Lighter at approximately **716 grams**, making it easier to handle for extended periods or during dynamic shooting scenarios.

- **FX3**: Heavier at around **646 grams**, which may provide a more stable feel but can be cumbersome for handheld shooting.

7. Price Point

- The FX30 is generally more affordable than the FX3, making it an attractive option for filmmakers on a budget who still want professional-quality video capabilities.

8. Video Bitrate and Recording Options

- **FX30**: Maximum video bitrate of up to **500 Mbps**, suitable for most video projects but slightly less than the FX3.
- **FX3**: Supports higher bitrates up to **600 Mbps**, allowing for better quality in demanding recording situations.

The choice between the Sony FX30 and FX3 largely depends on specific needs:

- The **FX30** is ideal for those who prioritize high-resolution stills, lighter weight, and cost-effectiveness while still offering strong video capabilities.
- The **FX3**, with its full-frame sensor, superior low-light performance, enhanced autofocus system, and higher continuous shooting speed, is better suited for professional filmmakers who require maximum performance in diverse shooting conditions.

Ultimately, both cameras are excellent tools for filmmakers, but understanding these differences will help users select the one that best meets their creative needs and budget constraints.

Comparisons with Sony Alpha Series

The Sony FX30 is positioned within Sony's Cinema Line, but it also shares several features and functionalities with the Sony Alpha series of cameras. Below are key comparisons that highlight the differences and similarities between the FX30 and various models from the Alpha series, particularly focusing on the A7 III and A7S III.

1. Sensor Type and Size

- **FX30**: Utilizes a **26.1 MP APS-C BSI CMOS sensor**. This sensor size offers a crop factor of 1.5x, which can be advantageous for certain types of shooting, such as wildlife or sports, where longer effective focal lengths are beneficial.
- **A7 III**: Features a **24.2 MP Full-Frame BSI CMOS sensor**, providing a wider field of view and superior low-light performance due to larger pixel sizes.
- **A7S III**: Equipped with a **12.1 MP Full-Frame BSI CMOS sensor**, optimized for video with exceptional low-light capabilities and dynamic range.

2. Video Capabilities

- **FX30**: Supports 4K recording at up to **120 fps** with 10-bit 4:2:2 colour depth, making it suitable for high-quality cinematic productions. It also offers S-Cinetone and S-Log3 profiles for enhanced colour grading flexibility.
- **A7 III**: Records 4K video but is limited to 8-bit colour depth and lacks advanced video features like S-Cinetone. It can shoot at up to **60 fps** in 4K.

- **A7S III**: Excels in video recording with capabilities for 4K at up to **120 fps**, similar to the FX30, but also supports 16-bit RAW output via HDMI, providing greater flexibility for professional workflows.

3. Autofocus System

- **FX30**: Features a fast hybrid autofocus system with **495 phase-detection points**, offering reliable tracking capabilities, including Real-time Eye AF for humans and animals.
- **A7 III**: Also has a hybrid AF system but with fewer phase-detection points (693), which may result in slightly slower performance compared to the FX30 in certain scenarios.
- **A7S III**: Boasts an advanced autofocus system with improved algorithms, allowing for faster and more accurate tracking than both the FX30 and A7 III.

4. Stills Photography

- **FX30**: Primarily designed as a cinema camera, it can capture stills at 26.1 MP but lacks continuous shooting modes (only single shots), which limits its utility for high-speed photography.
- **A7 III**: Excellent for still photography with continuous shooting up to **10 fps**, making it versatile for capturing action shots.
- **A7S III**: While primarily a video camera, it can also take high-quality stills but is not optimized for this purpose compared to the A7 III.

5. Build and Ergonomics

- **FX30**: Designed for video production, featuring a rugged body with multiple mounting points for accessories and an active cooling system for extended recording sessions.
- **A7 III & A7S III**: Both have compact designs suitable for handheld use, but they lack some of the dedicated video-centric features found on the FX30.

6. Price Point

- The FX30 is generally more affordable than the A7S III while providing many professional video features, making it an attractive option for filmmakers on a budget.
- The A7 III is often priced similarly to the FX30 but caters more towards hybrid shooters who need strong still photography capabilities alongside video.

The choice between the Sony FX30 and models from the Alpha series largely depends on specific needs:

- The **FX30** is ideal for filmmakers focused on video production who require high-quality features like high frame rates, advanced autofocus, and robust build quality tailored for cinema use.
- The **A7 III** serves as a versatile option for those who need strong performance in both stills and video but lacks some advanced video features.
- The **A7S III** is best suited for professionals seeking top-tier video performance in low-light conditions while still having solid stills capabilities.

Ultimately, each camera serves different purposes within the filmmaking spectrum, allowing users to choose based on their specific requirements and shooting styles.

Competitive Landscape: FX30 vs Other Brands

The Sony FX30 is a strong contender in the cinema camera market, positioned against various competitors from brands like Canon, Blackmagic, and Panasonic. This analysis will compare the FX30 with notable alternatives, focusing on their strengths and weaknesses.

1. **Sony FX30 vs Canon EOS R7**

   - **Sensor and Resolution**:
     - **FX30**: 26.1 MP APS-C BSI CMOS sensor.
     - **EOS R7**: 32.5 MP APS-C sensor, offering higher resolution for still photography.
   - **Video Capabilities**:
     - **FX30**: Records 4K up to **120 fps** in 10-bit 4:2:2, with options for S-Cinetone and S-Log3 for enhanced colour grading.
     - **R7**: Supports 4K up to **60 fps**, but with a crop factor in some modes, which can limit wide-angle shots.
   - **Autofocus**:
     - Both cameras feature advanced autofocus systems, but the FX30's Real-time Eye AF is particularly beneficial for video applications.
   - **Price Point**:
     - The R7 is generally priced lower than the FX30, making it a more budget-friendly option for hybrid shooters who also prioritize still photography.
   - **Conclusion**: The FX30 excels in video features and dynamic range, while the R7 offers superior still photography capabilities and slightly better image quality out of the camera.

2. **Sony FX30 vs Blackmagic Pocket Cinema Camera 6K Pro**

   - **Sensor Type**:
     - **FX30**: APS-C sensor.
     - **Blackmagic Pocket Cinema Camera 6K Pro**: Super 35 sensor with a resolution of up to **6144 x 3456**, providing higher resolution options for cinematic productions.
   - **Video Recording Formats**:
     - **FX30**: Offers high bitrate recording (10-bit) and RAW output via HDMI.
     - **Blackmagic**: Records in Blackmagic RAW and ProRes formats, known for their flexibility in post-production but lacks built-in stabilization.

- **Price Point**:
  - The FX30 is priced around **$1,800**, while the Pocket Cinema Camera typically costs more due to its advanced features like built-in ND filters.
- **Conclusion**: The FX30 is better suited for run-and-gun shooting due to its autofocus and usability, while the Blackmagic camera excels in resolution and colour science for controlled environments.

3. **Sony FX30 vs Panasonic Lumix GH6**
   - **Sensor Size**:
     - **FX30**: APS-C sensor.
     - **GH6**: Micro Four Thirds sensor, which provides a greater crop factor but allows for smaller lenses.
   - **Video Performance**:
     - **FX30**: Strong low-light performance with support for high frame rates.
     - **GH6**: Offers advanced video features including V-Log recording and high frame rate options (up to **300 fps in HD**), making it suitable for creative projects.
   - **Price Point**:
     - The GH6 is similarly priced to the FX30 but may offer more features for videographers focused on high frame rates.
   - **Conclusion**: The GH6 is ideal for users needing extensive video features in a compact form factor, while the FX30 excels in overall image quality and dynamic range.

Summary of Competitive Advantages

1. **Video Quality and Features**:
   - The FX30 stands out with its ability to record high bitrates (10-bit) and offers advanced colour science (S-Cinetone), making it suitable for professional video production.
2. **Usability and Design**:
   - With ergonomic design tailored for video shooting, including customizable buttons and extensive connectivity options (XLR inputs), the FX30 is well-suited for filmmakers who prioritize functionality.
3. **Price-to-Performance Ratio**:
   - Positioned as a more affordable option within Sony's cinema lineup, the FX30 provides significant value compared to similarly priced competitors that may not offer the same level of video-centric features.

The Sony FX30 holds a competitive position among various brands in the cinema camera market. Its combination of high-quality imaging, advanced video capabilities, and user-friendly design makes it an appealing choice for filmmakers looking to enhance their production quality without investing in higher-priced full-frame options.

While competitors like Canon and Blackmagic offer unique strengths, the FX30's balance of features positions it as a strong contender for both amateur and professional videographers.

CHAPTER TWELVE
PROS AND CONS

Advantages of the FX30

The Sony FX30 offers a range of features that make it an attractive option for filmmakers and content creators. Here are the key advantages of this digital cinema camera:

1. High-Quality Imaging

- **26.1 MP APS-C Sensor**: The FX30 is equipped with a back-illuminated Exmor R CMOS sensor, which provides excellent low-light performance and a wide dynamic range of **14 stops**. This allows for capturing detailed images in various lighting conditions, enhancing creative possibilities
- **6K Oversampling for 4K Output**: The camera utilizes 6K oversampling to produce high-quality UHD 4K video (3840 x 2160) with remarkable detail and clarity, making it suitable for professional-grade productions

2. Advanced Video Capabilities

- **High Frame Rates**: The FX30 supports recording in 4K at up to **120 fps** and Full HD at up to **240 fps**, enabling smooth slow-motion footage that adds dramatic effect to videos
- **Various Recording Formats**: It offers multiple recording formats, including XAVC HS and XAVC S-I, allowing for flexibility in post-production and ensuring high-quality output with options for 10-bit 4:2:2 colour depth

3. Professional Features

- **S-Cinetone Colour Science**: The camera incorporates S-Cinetone, which delivers pleasing skin tones and natural mid-tones right out of the camera, reducing the need for extensive colour grading in post-production
- **Dual Base ISO**: With dual base ISO settings of **800 and 2500**, the FX30 optimizes image quality in both bright and low-light environments, minimizing noise while maximizing dynamic range

4. Autofocus Performance

- **Fast Hybrid AF System**: The FX30 features a sophisticated autofocus system with **495 phase-detection points**, ensuring quick and accurate focusing across the frame. It includes Real-time Eye AF for tracking subjects' eyes, which is especially beneficial for portrait and wildlife videography
- **Focus Map and Breathing Compensation**: These features enhance manual focus control by visualizing depth of field and minimizing focus shift during rack focusing, respectively

5. User-Friendly Design

- **Compact and Lightweight**: Weighing just **1.2 lbs**, the FX30 is designed for handheld use without needing a cage, making it ideal for on-the-go shooting

- **Customizable Controls**: The camera offers customizable buttons and an intuitive menu system that allows users to quickly access frequently used settings, streamlining the shooting process

6. Robust Connectivity Options

- **HDMI Output**: The full-size HDMI port supports 16-bit RAW output to external recorders, enabling high-quality capture for demanding workflows
- **Audio Inputs**: With a 3.5mm microphone input and optional XLR handle unit support, the FX30 caters to professional audio needs, ensuring high-quality sound capture alongside

The Sony FX30 stands out as a versatile digital cinema camera that combines high-quality imaging with advanced video capabilities and user-friendly features. Its robust design, professional functionalities, and excellent autofocus system make it an ideal choice for both aspiring filmmakers and seasoned professionals looking to create stunning visual content.

Potential Limitations and Workarounds

While the Sony FX30 is a robust camera with many advantages, it does have some limitations that users should be aware of. Here's a summary of these potential drawbacks along with suggested workarounds.

1. Rolling Shutter

Limitation: The FX30 exhibits noticeable rolling shutter effects, especially during fast pans or quick movements, which can lead to distortion in moving subjects. This is particularly evident compared to higher-end models like the FX3 or A7S III, which have faster sensor readout times

Workaround:

- **Use Stabilization**: Enable In-Body Image Stabilization (IBIS) to help reduce micro jitters and improve overall footage stability.
- **Limit Fast Movements**: When possible, avoid rapid camera movements or use slower pans to minimize rolling shutter effects.

2. Low Light Performance

Limitation: The FX30 has two base ISOs (800 and 2500), which may feel limiting compared to full-frame cameras that offer a more significant jump in exposure. Users may find it challenging to achieve optimal low-light performance, especially in 4K at high frame rates

Workaround:

- **Proper Lighting Setup**: Invest in good lighting equipment to enhance shooting conditions. This can significantly alleviate low-light challenges.
- **Use Fast Lenses**: Incorporate fast prime lenses with larger apertures to improve light intake.

3. Lack of Internal ND Filters

Limitation: The absence of built-in neutral density (ND) filters means users must rely on external filters for controlling exposure in bright conditions, which can add complexity and weight to setups

Workaround:

- **Use High-Quality External ND Filters**: Invest in a set of high-quality ND filters that can be easily mounted on your lenses for flexibility in various lighting conditions.

4. Limited Frame Rate Options in PAL Mode

Limitation: In PAL mode, the FX30 only offers 50p and 100p frame rates, while switching to NTSC mode allows for additional options like 24p and 60p. This limitation can be frustrating for users shooting in regions that typically use PAL standards

Workaround:

- **Switch to NTSC Mode**: If your project allows it, switch the camera to NTSC mode for greater frame rate flexibility. Just be cautious about potential flickering issues with certain artificial lights when shooting at different frame rates.

5. No Built-in Shutter Angle Control

Limitation: The FX30 lacks advanced features like shutter angle settings, which are common in higher-end cinema cameras. This can limit precise control over motion blur

Workaround:

- **Manual Shutter Speed Adjustment**: Use the manual shutter speed setting to approximate desired motion blur based on frame rate (e.g., using a shutter speed of 1/50s for 24p).

6. Ergonomics and Button Placement

Limitation: Some users find the joystick placement on the top of the camera less ergonomic compared to other models like the A7S III, making it less intuitive for adjusting focus points

Workaround:

- **Practice and Adaptation**: Spend time familiarizing yourself with the button layout and joystick functionality. Consider using a cage or handle that provides better grip and access to controls.

While the Sony FX30 has its limitations, understanding these challenges allows users to implement effective workarounds that enhance their shooting experience. By utilizing proper lighting, external accessories, and adapting shooting techniques, filmmakers can maximize the potential of this capable camera.

Ideal Use Cases for Different Filmmakers

The Sony FX30 is a versatile cinema camera that caters to various filmmakers, from beginners to seasoned professionals. Its features make it suitable for a wide range of applications. Here are some ideal use cases for different types of filmmakers:

1. **Aspiring Filmmakers and Content Creators**

- **YouTube and Online Content**: The FX30 is perfect for YouTubers and online content creators looking to produce high-quality videos without breaking the bank. Its ability to shoot 4K at up to 120 fps allows for cinematic slow-motion effects, which are popular in many online video formats

- **Vlogs and Personal Projects**: The compact design and lightweight nature of the FX30 make it an excellent choice for vlogging or personal projects, where mobility and ease of use are essential.

2. Wedding and Event Videographers

- **Weddings**: The camera's small form factor and high-quality audio capabilities (with optional XLR inputs) make it ideal for capturing weddings and events. Its dual base ISO (800/2500) helps maintain good image quality in varying lighting conditions, which is crucial during ceremonies
- **Corporate Events**: Videographers can utilize the FX30 for corporate functions, where a professional appearance and high-quality footage are required. The camera's ability to record in 10-bit 4:2:2 ensures that the final product meets client expectations.

3. Wildlife and Nature Filmmakers

- **Wildlife Filming**: The FX30's APS-C sensor provides a crop factor that effectively extends the reach of full-frame lenses, making it advantageous for wildlife filmmakers who need to capture distant subjects

Additionally, its fast autofocus system with animal tracking capabilities enhances the ability to capture moving subjects accurately.

4. B-Camera Operators

- **Film Sets**: For filmmakers working on larger productions, the FX30 serves as an excellent B-camera option. Its ability to match the quality of higher-end cameras like the FX3 makes it suitable for capturing secondary angles or behind-the-scenes footage

This flexibility allows operators to contribute effectively without needing a separate high-end camera.

5. Live Streamers and Podcasters

- **Live Streaming**: The FX30 can be employed as a live streaming camera due to its USB-C capabilities, allowing for direct connection to streaming software and high-quality audio capture

This is particularly useful for podcasters or content creators who want professional-grade video quality during live sessions.

6. Educational Purposes

- **Film Schools and Workshops**: The FX30 is an excellent choice for educational institutions teaching filmmaking due to its combination of professional features and user-friendly interface. It allows students to learn about cinematography without the intimidation of more complex systems

7. Short Films and Independent Projects

- **Indie Filmmakers**: Independent filmmakers can leverage the FX30's high-quality image capture, dynamic range, and colour science (including S-Cinetone) to produce visually compelling short films or narrative projects on a budget

The Sony FX30 is an adaptable tool that meets the needs of various filmmakers across different genres. Whether it's creating engaging online content, capturing significant life events, or producing independent films, the FX30 offers professional features at an accessible price point, making it a valuable asset in any filmmaker's toolkit.

THANK YOU FOR READING

www.ingramcontent.com/pod-product-compliance
Lightning Source LLC
Chambersburg PA
CBHW082252220526
45469CB00009B/2979